SILENCE BROKEN

AFTER 50 YEARS

PRINCE EDWARD COUNTY

1959 - 1964

By
Rita Odom Moseley

Book Design and Cover
by The Creative Short Book Writers Project
Wayne Drumheller, Editor and Founder
Printing Platform: KDP Amazon.com.

ISBN: 13: 978-1092580328

To: Florence

Book paid for - courtesy of my
niece Dr. Latifa Odom Silski.

— Rita Odom Moseley

Authors Disclaimer

Dedicated to the Memory of my Mother
January 2, 1924-December 20, 1987
Rosa Margaret Foster-Odom

Contents

Author's Introduction

Before The School Closed

When I think back to before the school closing in Prince Edward County; Farmville was a small quiet little town on the cusp of growth and prosperity. It was an ideal community to raise a family, or start a small business. There was a large number of Black owned businesses in the town of Farmville that stretched from one end of Main Street to the other, as well as throughout the county. It was considered normal during that time for neighborhoods to be separated by race. The schools were separated under the pretense that they were "separate but equal," following the law passed and set in place by Plessy v Ferguson in 1896. That however, could not have been further from the truth. This was the first indicator and yet no one knew that our quiet little town was about to change forever. It was as if all of a sudden, you could see within the distance an ominous storm heading our way.

This was the beginning of resistance; a simple humble request for a better and equal school for Blacks. The High School for Black children were without the necessary equipment, books, and space needed for classrooms. The capacity of the building was overflowing. It stood in stark contrast of the White children's school; which was a brick two story building, equipped with all the necessary resources for a proper learning environment. They had what we did not. This changed when young Barbara Rose Johns decided to do something about it.

FOREWORD

In writing this piece I asked my schoolmates to tell their stories during the closing of the public schools for five years in Prince Edward County. Some were reluctant to talk after 60 years. I was directly affected myself; I understand the pain that still lingers. I felt their stories would be informative, but I didn't realize how much history would be told. I realized that they not only had a story to tell, but they had a story that needed to be told for themselves. I had no idea what a phenomenal thing I had come across. Shortly after beginning the interviews, I realized this book did something that no one had done for this population of children (now adults) within 50 years.

It was an amazing finding. This platform gave many of my schoolmates a first-time opportunity to relieve themselves of so much pain and sometime bitterness that had been bottled up for all of those years. Many of them told their story for the first time, many of them had never contemplated ever telling their story to anyone. What I found out as I was listening to them, or reading their stories they had given me, was the miraculous thing that was occurring before my eyes. For so many of my schoolmates, telling their stories was a relief, but most importantly, a therapeutic mechanism that I had given them without knowing it would occur. I know this because I could see the transformation of many emotions as they were telling their story. I have been told by many that after 50 years, it was a great burden lifted off of them to talk or write about it. Throughout my interviews I felt over and over again the anguish, pain and forgiveness eliminated or subsided. I was able to administer therapy for them and myself without being aware of it until it occurred, and that, I am most proud.

I see this as history. I have always believed that if you don't know your past you will not recognize it when it returns, having the same effect, but with another name. I found that this book gave the therapeutic element that was never given, and displayed the ability, in spite of what and how this event occurred, the survival skills of each of us. The closing of the schools was a tragedy, but there were some who felt that it gave them opportunities that they would never have gotten. In these stories readers will see growth and forgiveness.

Rita Odom-Moseley

I was in the sixth grade when the school closed. I found out about the school closing from friends. We were not happy about it. I loved school and I loved learning; therefore, a lot was taken away from me when my education was denied. I don't remember my mother ever talking about the school closing; therefore, I drew my own conclusion of why it had closed.

I lived yards from Mary E Branch #1 Elementary School and the Mary E. Branch #2 Middle School that was across the street from the Elementary School, both schools I attended. Therefore I walked to my elementary and middle school until school closed.

My family walked everywhere because my mother never owned a car. I walked to my school, while she walked to Longwood College, (University) where she worked in the laundry room. We frequently used bags of coal in the winter for heating while my brother pulled the little red wagon behind us to bring the heavy bag home. We shopped down town Farmville businesses when we had to purchase items the Black owned stores did not carry.

My mother left me with my grandmother while she worked. After she realized that school would not reopen, she put me in Brownie and Girl Scouts. She had no way to send me to another school. After being out of public school for two years, my Girl Scout leader asked my mother would she allow me to go away to school. Within a week, my mother and I were picked up by the Girl Scout leader, Mrs. Anna Mae Griggs, and Mrs. Styles who drove us to Blacksburg, Virginia. Prior to that day, I had never been away from home. My mother had never met the people I was to live with, they were strangers. When we arrived, two women were standing on the front porch waiting as we pulled in the drive way. I figured that the mother was nearing 100 years old and the daughter about 80. The daughter was Assistant Principal in Pulaski County, where she lived during the weekday and came home on the weekend.

Another student, Doris Williams a few years older than me also came to live with the Anderson family. I lived with the mother and walked to an all-Black one-room school, which had an accordion petition in the center to create two classrooms. At the end of that school year, I was chosen salutatorian of that graduating class, the second smartest. I give all the credit to my teachers who made sure I learned the basics and everything they taught me before our school closed.

The next year, I attended CII, Christiansburg Industrial Institute in Christiansburg, Virginia; a school of academic and vocational classes. This was my first experience of riding on a school bus. It was a huge adjustment for a little girl who lived in a small town and had only seen two schools each a single building her entire life. CII consisted of several buildings in a college style setting. There was a separate building for the office, the library, cosmetology, barber class and home economics in a single building. Gym, band and wood shop was in another building. There was a building for teaching typing and accounting, an academic building with classes such as math, history, science etc. The experience was so overwhelming that a lot of it has been blocked out. Taking a cosmetology class and being taught to play a beautiful Indian song on the piano were two of my fondest memories.

I was adjusting to Blacksburg and CII schools, but at the end of the second school year, I was told by the Anderson family that our schools would re-open in the fall. They gave me the option to continue to stay with them throughout my high school graduation, and in return they would send me to college. At that age, I did not know the significance of a college education. I knew no one personally that had gone to college, so the most important thing to me was to go home with my family and especially my brother, whom I had left behind. Of course, now, I know that would have been a life transformation for me.

In 1963, I returned home to attend the Free School that would transition us back into the public-school setting. I wanted so badly to take piano lessons when I returned home. Of course, we did not own a piano, and my mother could not afford to pay Mrs. Madison for piano lessons. It was far beyond my reach and my passion for playing a piano died.

The following year the public schools officially reopened. I attended Robert R. Moton High School and graduated two years later than I should have due to the closing. During my senior year, after getting out of school at 3:00 pm. I worked until 12:00 mid-night.

Looking back, one thing I never forgot when I lived in Blacksburg was Mrs. Anderson's Grace before meals. "Dear Lord, Bless the food I am about to receive and let it nourish my body from time to time for my redeemer's sake. Amen." I use to wonder, who is my redeemer's sake? Even though I didn't' know what redeemer's sake meant, that grace remained with me throughout my entire life.

I don't know what I would have been if school had not closed but based on what I have accomplished at this late stage of my life, I believe I would have accomplished something greater. It's no longer painful to think about what I could have done, or whom I could have become, but the scars as a young girl will forever be with me. I use to blame the white kids for our schools being closed, until I was old enough to know that it was not their choice, but the choice of their parents and others.

I am not angry or bitter about what happened to me. Not being angry was a conscious choice I made. I didn't want to transfer negative feelings to my kids; I saw too much of that. I told my children what happened when I felt they were old enough to separate the bad feelings of my experience from the history it told.

I retired in 2013 after working 35 years for Prince Edward County Public School System. Before I applied for employment in our school system, I worked nine years at Craddock Terry Shoe factory immediately after graduating from high school. There were few places a young Black girl would be hired in our town, except for the obvious, and I decided not to go that route, I tried that when I was twelve. Craddock Terry was also convenient because it was in walking distance. I also worked 2 years at CPAC Head Start Program in Cumberland, Virginia, about 20 miles from home,

When the Brown Scholarship was signed into law, I enrolled in Saint Paul's College in 2005 and earned my Bachelor of Science Degree in Business Administration. I will forever be grateful to Saint Paul's College, the staff and their professors. If not for them coming to us and the Brown Scholarship providing the funding, I would not have gotten the opportunity to further my education. I felt that would satisfy my desire for education and make my deceased mother proud. One year later, I had the strongest aspiration to continue my education. I enrolled at Liberty University in 2010, and earned my Master of Arts in Human Services and Executive Leadership Degree in 2013. Both were funded through the Brown Scholarship which provided free tuition for anyone directly affected by the closing of the schools and lived in the state of Virginia. Even though I contemplated it, and was approved for the funding, a number of things deterred me from pursuing my Doctorate Degree. My lifelong ambition has been to write and get published the many books I had in my head. I am currently writing my fourth book to date. In addition to reading and writing, I enjoy collecting stamps and money from other countries.

I feel that many of the decisions we made, would not have occurred at such a young age, if the school had not been closed for so many years. I am proud that through it all, many continued their education, but there were still many that did not. I am proud of them too, because they survived it all.

What I am most proud of in addition to fulfilling my mother's educational dream, are my two children, JoAnn and Frank, II and my granddaughter Bryonna.

If anyone ever wondered what I think about my town, Farmville, in Prince Edward County, Virginia, where I still reside, the answer is quite simple, I love the town. The past is to be remembered as history, and not relived. This place is so much like me, not perfect, but enough perfection, it's still small, but growing in size, peaceful, and growing in respect for others and that gives me so much comfort.

The children of the Massive Resistance stories cannot be told without recognizing the historical event of sixteen-year-old Barbara Rose Johns. In 1951, she and her classmates led an all children's strike, a full eight years prior to the closing of Prince Edward County Schools. There have been many works written about this historical event, including the Virginia Civil Rights Memorial erected in 2008, therefore I will not go into any great detail discussing it.

I will focus this book on the oral histories of the students who were locked out of their public school for five years. During the course of my research, however, I was able to interview a few people that lived through that experience of the strike area. Barbara's sister Joan Johns Cobbs, Joy Cabarrus, and Louis Taylor Eanes recall their firsthand account.

A WELL-PLANNED STRIKE

Events Occurred Before the Necessity for the Training Centers

Joan Marie Johns-Cobbs

Joan tells her sister's story of how she remembered the Historical Strike in Prince Edward County. "I was in the 8th grade - 13 yrs. old when my sister, Barbara Johns staged that historical walkout on September 23, 1951. I was attending Robert Russa Moton High School on that day, and I was at school in the auditorium. My sister was prompted to take such an endeavor as to call a strike because of inadequate facilities at the school; no science labs, no gym, no cafeteria, tattered and used books, etc.

13

Barbara Rose Johns Barbara felt that her plan was divinely inspired since she had prayed to God for help. So, she assembled student council members that she trusted, and they met in secret and formulated plans for the strike. She was able to gather the students in the auditorium by

forging Principal Jones' initials on a letter sent to the teachers. I feel that Barbara may have been influenced by our uncle Vernon Johns since she had many of his characteristics: outspoken, determined, fearless, courageous, brave, sincere and religious.

Barbara was a Librarian in Public Schools in Philadelphia, Pennsylvania. She was 56 years old when she died on September 25, 1991.

Joy Cabarrus Speakes talks about the era of the historical student strike.

My Experience as a striker in the April 23, 1951 Student Strike. Plaintiff in Davis v. County School Board of Prince Edward County, one of the five cases combined into Brown v. Board of Education.

I lived in Darlington Heights Virginia, in a home that my grandfather built, with my grandparents George P. Morton and Emma H. Morton. I attended Robert Russa Moton High School located in Farmville, VA about 16 miles from where I lived. My principal before school closed was Mr. S. F. Griffin. When we went on strike the principal was Mr. Boyd Jones. My father, Henry W. Cabarrus was a Longshoreman and my mother was a nurse. I graduated in 1955 so I was not attending school when the schools closed.

The Robert Russa Moton High School was built in 1939 by Martha E. Forrester Council of Women to hold 180 African American students. In 1951 there were over 400 students attending the school. Our parents had been attending the PTA meetings, school board, and visiting Superintendent T. J. McIlwaine's office with no success in getting a new school building. We had no cafeteria, no gym, and no lab. They gave us three Tar Paper shacks made like chicken coups instead of a new school. They had a big potbelly stove and if you were setting near the stove you had to take your coats and sweaters off, but if you were setting near the door you had to keep your coats on and when it rained you had to put up an umbrella so that your paper that you were taking notes on did not get wet.

All of the buses were second hand and some students took classes in buses. Two teachers would be teaching in the auditorium different subjects at the same time. Can you imagine trying to concentrate! The conditions were deplorable that we had to endure. The books that we received had pages torn out, vulgar racial statements and epitaphs in them. All of the teachers we had were great, they gave 110% because they wanted to make sure that we continued our education.

Barbara became very frustrated with the overcrowded and inferior conditions at the school. Mrs. Inez Jones, Barbara's music teacher, was her favorite teacher. One day she said to Mrs. Jones that something had to be done about the deplorable condition that we endured and Mrs. Jones said to her "Then do something about it". At the time Barbara did not understand why she gave her that answer, but it was because she could not tell her what to do. Her job would be in jeopardy if she gave her advice.

Barbara began to put a plan together with a committee of students that she felt she could trust to execute the plan. Barbara took care of her siblings because her mother worked in Washington, D.C. One day they all went to wait for the bus and Barbara realized that she had left her lunch home. She went back home to get her lunch and when she returned the bus was gone. There she was on the side of the road hoping and praying that someone would pass and take her to school. The white school bus passed and they could not pick her up because she was African American. This angered Barbara. The next thing that upset her was the school bus accident that occurred in March at Elam Crossing in Prospect, Virginia where five students were killed. They were all from the same family and one of them was Barbara's best friend.

Those two incidents made Barbara put her plan into action immediately. On April 23, 1951 I went to school and it seemed like any other day but it was very different, it was the beginning of a 13-year struggle for equal rights in public education. Barbara had John Watson go downtown and make a call back to principal Jones and tell him that some students were downtown at the bus station creating a problem. Barbara knew that when Mr. Jones got the call, he would leave immediately. Mr. Jones was very strict and always instructed all students that they represented Robert Russa Moton High School, the community and they were not to get out of order at school or in the community.

When Barbara got the signal that Mr. Jones had left the building, she went into action sending a note to all classrooms to come to the auditorium. The note was signed B.J., her initials, which were the same as initials of Boyd Jones, the principal.

When we all arrived in the auditorium and the curtains opened, there was Barbara Johns on the stage with John Stokes and his twin sister Carrie Stokes. We were all in shock except the ones that were on her planning committee. Barbara asked all of the teachers to leave the auditorium because she did not want them to get in trouble. Most of the teachers left and the ones that refused Barbara had some football players escort them out. None of the teachers knew of the plan.

Barbara started to speak, telling us that we did not have to accept the deplorable conditions that we were exposed to, her sister Joan was three seats in front of me and she kept sliding down in her seat because she did not know what Barbara was going to say next. I know that it was divine intervention because after Barbara said that a little child should lead.

One student stood up and said "What if we are all put in Jail." Barbara replied, "The jail is not big enough to hold all of us." She also said in a very firm voice "We will go out on strike and stay out until we get a new school."

John Stokes stood up and started to chant, "one bit, two bits, all in favor of the strike holler." All of the students, over 400, began to walk out of the auditorium to go on strike. Some went downtown to the superintendent's office, some held up signs on the grounds and some went home. I went home and was more afraid of what my grandparents would say when I told them that Barbara Johns had led over 400 students out of the school and we were on strike. As expected, my grandmother was not pleased. She was a school teacher and we were taught not to rebel or disrespect our teachers, elders or individuals that we were under their supervision. My grandfather was in support because he was a civil rights activist and had been attending many meetings with Otis Scott trying to get a new school for the African American students that was equal to the white school. The high school for whites was only a few blocks from the school for African American students but the difference was as if it was in another country.

I knew Rev. Griffin because my Aunt Etta Lee and her husband attended First Baptist Church. He was a shepherd to us when the students went on strike. He let us use the basement of the church for meetings and made calls to parents urging them to support the students. I graduated from the new Robert Russa High School in 1955. This school was built in 1953 with hopes that the NAACP would drop the case. I was living in New York so I was not affected by the school closing, but my Brother, Henry Cabarrus, was. The April 23, 1951 student strike led by Barbara Rose Johns made the Robert Russa Moton High School the birthplace of the Civil Rights Movement. The strike preceded Rosa Parks, Martin Luther King, Ruby Bridges and many other Civil Rights movements. There would not have been a case if Barbara Rose Johns and Carrie Stokes had not written a letter to the NAACP and insisted that the lawyers come to Farmville and meet with them. The School Board closed the school for five years to keep from integrating.

I want people to remember me as an advocate of equality and rights for all human beings regardless of ethnicity or gender; one of the students that walked out with Barbara Rose Johns on April 23, 1951 and a plaintiff in the Davis vs. Prince Edward County Board of Education, one of the five cases in the Brown vs. Board of Education. I moved to New York and attended New York University, but did not graduate. I worked for Magic Marker Corporation for over 35 years; Became Sales Director, Member of the Board of Directors and Secretary of Magic Marker. I retired and returned to Virginia in 2007 where I am a member of Triumph Church, the NAACP, serve on the Robert Russa Moton Council, Moton Trustee Board, Prince Edward Democratic Committee and the Family Challenge Development Chair. My skills are marketing, public relations and fundraising.

Louis Taylor Eanes

I was living at home with my parents and attending Robert R. Moton High School in 1951. I was one of the students during the walkout. Barbara Johns approached me and told me that there would be no school tomorrow. I asked her a question, why, she just said, look, you will find out later, but there is no school tomorrow, and that's when we separated, that's all I found out that day. Next two or three-days things kinda gathered about we were on a strike, a walk out. No attending school for better school. We won't be going to school for better schools, that's what I was told in the next three days. I wasn't in the walk out, when I came home that evening, she told me. I told my father that there is no school tomorrow.

Well, naturally he wanted to know why. I told him, I don't know daddy, we don't go to school and at that time a lot of farming was going on. He was kinda glad to see me at home (he laughed) for a couple days with the farm work, tobacco, corn whatever we were raising at the time. I didn't do any walking out as far as the walking; I just stayed at home the next day. It was kinda kept like a secret. The principal wasn't supposed to know anything about it, or he would have gotten fired. It was done like students were doing it, now how it was really done, I don't know. I heard a lot of different things but it was done without the teachers and all knowing about it or they would have gotten fired.

I didn't feel bad of that nature, I thought they did a good thing until the school was closed and that time I say um, that walk out is what caused the school to close, I just felt a little guilty, not bad, kinda thinking I did the right thing and kinda thinking I did the wrong thing, but after all in this life now, I think that I did do the right thing. Now the guilt has kinda left. It was 21 of us and at that time I had graduated and I really didn't pay too much mind by being young, I didn't really realize, seem to me, just how important education was, I just thinking well, they will make it in life and didn't realize, but after I grew older, a few years older, I realize what a bad thing that was done. School closing, no education you know and I had graduated from Moton in 1952 and I was thinking about my brothers and sisters, no education, some of them can't read, or write.

I had classes in the tar papered shack, you know it was a little cold in the winter time and hot in the summer time when it turns warm, you know it just wasn't adequate heat and air condition and things like they have today. No cafeteria was in the tar papered shack. In some part of the day, I had classes in the school. There is much improvement in the schools today than when I was going to school, school buses and classrooms are better also.

I just like to say, I can speak for my family and some other families that's kinda close, I know, would like to say this, that God will make a way. I would have thought that it would have been much tougher on my family going through life and trying to get a start in life without schooling, but all of them survived some kind of way, you know, can read some, write, they don't have a college degree, maybe, but it sat them back some in their education, but they was able to get right good jobs, work on their own, a couple brothers are brick layers, that was in the school closing, different types of work and owned their own businesses, so God survived them. You would be surprised how advanced I think that they made without an education. We got together and did brick mason and carpentry so we could do our own work. Most of us built our own homes with the help of one another. It's just a little bit of a gift of carpentry that runs in the family and it come from some on my mother's side and a little bit on my father's side.

The strike came as a surprise to all and ended up being a significant game changer in the resistance movement. Parents were not told of plans of the strike and the Principal of the Black children's school had no knowledge of it.

Leslie L. Hall

Mr. Leslie Hall was interviewed in 2008, at the age of 100. Mr. L. L. Hall, as he was called by everyone, was Prince Edward County Public school's Principal before they closed the schools for five years in 1959. He passed in December 2012. He tells the process of how he was not rehired for the school system and why.

I came here after I was out of the army, in 1942.

I became principal of both buildings, Mary E. Branch 1 Elementary School and the Mary E. Branch 2 Middle School. I didn't have a secretary in either office

When I asked Mr. Hall if he knew about Barbara Johns' and Reverend Griffin's meetings, he stated, "I didn't know anything about the school, he and Barbara kept it quiet." I didn't actually know anything about the walk out. Ms. Johnson who taught the 6th and 7th grade, said come look at this, I bet you have never seen anything like it. I was standing upstairs in Ms. Johnson's classroom and I saw the parade of children marching down the street.

When asked what he was doing at the onset of the school closing he replied, "I was trying to get out of the way of everything. I had two children school age at that time. Crawley was the baby, the schools were to open in September, and he never got a chance to go to school in Prince Edward. He enrolled into Cumberland Schools. Brother Leslie Junior was in the 6th grade, Tooty was in the 8th grade, I had those two, they didn't know where they were going.

I went for a job near Fredericksburg. A friend of mine in the NAACP called me and told me you got to get down here. I did not come back after schools were opened, they wanted me to come back as a new teacher, as a new person and I was ready to sign the contract and he said no, Mr. Hall, you got to come back as a new person, or you can't come back. I had 22, 23 years in and I had to come back as a new teacher? I stayed in Cumberland.

James Bash
1924 – 2014

James Bash was Principal of the White children's school before the Prince Edward County Schools closed in 1959. He was a devoted educator and passionate activist. He served the Commonwealth as a supporter of civil rights and desegregation efforts in the 1950s and 1960s. While serving as the principal of the White High School in Farmville in 1955, Mr. Bash courageously stepped out on Longwood College's auditorium stage at a meeting of co-workers and community and spoke out against plans to prevent desegregation of the school. He was immediately mistreated and disrespected by friends and co-workers. He moved to Charlottesville and secured a federal grant to fund the Consultative Resource Center for School Desegregation he founded at the Curry School of Education at the University of Virginia. Due to the recognition of exceptional leadership of the Consultative Resource Center for School Desegregation and many contributions to the Commonwealth, James Bash was named a professor emeritus of the Curry School of Education. He retired in 1991. On March 7, 2014, he received a resolution from the General Assembly, for his service as an educator, an activist for civil rights and desegregation and for his work to ensure equality for all citizens of the Commonwealth.

A Conversation with Mr. Lester Andrews - School Board Chairman, 1959-2008

At the time of this interview, Mr. Lester Andrews was one of the owners of Andrews, Large and Whitten. He was 39 years old when school closed and 89 years old when I interviewed him. He was the School Board's Chairman in Prince Edward County at the time of the school closing. I was given this interview because I told him that I would write a book. He invited me into his office for this interview.

His first statement before I asked a question was: The school board didn't have any input in the closing of the schools. The Board of supervisors cut money off for the schools.

I asked Mr. Andrews how he felt about the decision to close the schools in Prince Edward County, he said "I was against it."

When I asked if he was one of the white parents who went to the bank in the middle of the night to get checks or vouchers to be able to attend the all-white school, Prince Edward Academy, after it was built, he said, "No, I had two boys and they attended school at the Baptist Church, most of the schools were held in churches."

The deciding time to close the schools was the meeting at Longwood College. I was there, but I don't remember seeing any Blacks and I don't know if any Black families were notified, I was not a part of that group. Barry Wall, Mr. Glenn and Robert Taylor were.

I asked him if he spoke out against it. No, I never openly spoke out against it. It wasn't because I was afraid of the backlash from my community and the possibility of losing my business. No, it was not that I was afraid of my business so much, I kept quiet because of the relationship with the community and the concern I had for my children.

Mr. Andrews told me of several incidents that occurred during that era. The first was about one of his children; when he returned home from work one day his wife was upset and his son was crying. When he asked them what was wrong, they told him that their son was not invited to a birthday party because his father was on the school board and did not vote for the closing of the schools. He explained to his son that the school board did not have anything to do with the closing of the school.

Another incident he told me occurred in 1960 when he found out the Black community was going to boycott his business. He had about 63 Black employees at the time. He and the owners went to the community to talk to them and ask them not to boycott his business. They informed them that the school Board was not the ones who closed the schools and that the Board of Supervisors wouldn't fund it. Mr. Andrew stated that the Black community called it off.

The third occurrence was when he had planned a cruise with his family well ahead of time before the decision of the school closing. After he refused to go along with it, they did not allow his family to go on the cruise.

The school board members including himself as chairman were in place before the closing of the school decision. After the decision to close the schools every school board member left the school board except one and a new group came in. This is his story in his own words.

1951, after many unsuccessful attempts both by the parents and their children, to get the leaders of the community to help get a better school, a civil rights attorney from Richmond, Virginia, Oliver Hill Sr. was contacted. The strikers persuaded Oliver Hill, Sr. to come to Farmville, Virginia to help them. Above is a picture of me and two other Brown Scholars standing behind Mr. Hill in his home, with me holding the microphone while he was being interviewed. He was asked if he remembered the meetings he had in Farmville and if he recalled the terms in which he would agree to help. He told step by step exactly what occurred, from the time he was contacted to the day he came to Prince Edward, and spoke to the students and parents. He concluded that he would only take the case if they agreed to integrate the schools instead of fighting to make them equal to the white children's school. That was not what they wanted, but they all agreed to Mr. Hill's suggestion of fighting in courts to integrate. Mr. Hill and his team fought in the Supreme Court until the court decided to hear the Prince Edward case and demanded that the county reopen schools on a desegregated basis. At the time of this interview with Senator Henry Marsh, Mr. Hill was 100 years old and totally blind.

In 1959, chains were placed on the Farmville school doors with huge locks and the elementary school playground was stripped of all the children's favorite equipment except the tall metal sliding board.

Senator Henry Marsh

His journey to Prince Edward County

My sole intention in doing this interview was to find out what part Senator Marsh played in the Prince Edward County struggle. Here he tells his story.

 When I contacted Mr. Hill in May of 61, he was closing down his political office working for President John Kennedy and he told me I could return to Richmond. When I joined him in Richmond, he introduced me for the first time to Samuel W. Tucker. He informed us that President Kennedy had appointed him to a position in the Housing Administration under Robert Weaver and he would have to leave us for a few years and he would rejoin the firm at a later time. My supervisor hid me in a back room when the Kennedy representatives visited my job, until the Kennedy folks left, because I was black and had a law degree and was member of the bar and was on the GS4 with the White law students on the GS5, GS7 and GS9.

So, he put me in a GS4 Target 5, that's a federal legal job, but I was a lawyer and that is where I was when John Kennedy was elected, and he sent his team around to Liberty Loan Building where I was evaluating pension plans. And that's where I was in 59 when schools were closed. I kept in touch with Oliver and he was fighting Massive Resistance because Brown had been decided in 54-55 this was 59. That's what I was doing in 59.

After I did my six months, I came to Richmond and joined the firm and that's when I got a call from Oliver saying, Henry I need you to go to Prince Edward, I said what's wrong, he said my intern Fred Wallace was arrested in the courthouse for attacking the sheriff, and they will kill him if you don't get him out of there. That's how I got involved with Prince Edward after Massive Resistance. It took us five years to get Fred out of that mess. He was why I became a lawyer and became a representative for Griffin and the group that was supporting Griffin and my law firm became the law firm for the group, and I represented them for years, that's how I got to know you and others. That was my first experience when I came to get him out of jail, his name was Fred Wallace, yea, he would have been killed in that court house, because he called Sheriff Overton deputy, he called him by his real name, SOB, (laughed). They say he attacked him, but I think they attacked him. No, he didn't take no stuff, he was 250 pounds, a big man and he didn't like law enforcement people. He didn't take no stuff off them, so I was lucky to get him out of jail in one piece. That was my first experience down in Farmville. I was assigned to work with Griffin and his group, they met at First Baptist Church, and for years I represented them, and the Pastor Williams was pastor of First Baptist Church, he picketed the White church and they arrested him, all of that stuff was going on down there in Prince Edward. Yes, Oliver sent me down to go down and help Fred Wallace because he needed help.

When I heard about the closing, I was really upset, I was in Virginia Union in 1955 when the court decided the case and I was upset and I went out and testified on my own against their plan to change the constitution so they could use public funds for private schools. I was upset as a student, and there were 37 speakers and I was the one only youth and that's how I met Oliver Hill, he spoke against Massive Resistance representing Virginia State Conference and I spoke representing student government, and he came over to me and he said, boy that was a good speech, what you going to do when you grow up, I said I wanna come back and work with you. He said really, I said really, he said come on, shake hands, I give you a job, when you finish, you come on back and work for me. That's how while I was still in college, I got a job with the greatest Virginian of the Twentieth Century, Oliver Hill. When he got ready for me, he called me back and I came back and worked for his firm.

Yea, I was with Oliver Hill when he was fighting for Prince Edward County schools, but not initially, I met him when he testified against the Massive Resistance plans to change the constitution so the public funds could go to the private schools, that's how I met him, and we shook hands on the deal, but I wasn't a member of the firm, I was a student, I was going to law school. We kept in touch and I went to law school and we kept in touch, because I had a fiancée in Richmond, now my wife. I was coming to Richmond once a month to see her, and there were women in DC trying to get me, but they couldn't, I wasn't interested and we have been married 50 some years.

Parents and caretakers were not expecting the five-year closing of their public school. Many were unprepared for the split decisions they were forced to make. Should they keep their children at home or send them away to live with relatives, friends or strangers? Just think about that for a moment. Faced with an impossible choice; what would you have done? There were others who thought of innovative methods for their children to receive an education. This included using abandoned homes, traveling over county lines as well as moving themselves across the country with their children. This was a time of extreme adversity and I am always amazed with the fortitude people displayed as they quickly gathered the strength to survive it all.

Note: Throughout this book you will hear many talks about the Free School. The Free school to some were the Centers provided throughout the counties. That was understood because the centers provided practically the same curriculum as the public school. Therefore, those who speak of the Free School during the school closing are referring to the Centers. The actual Free School did not occur until the year school reopened.

After Prince Edward County Public Schools were closed, PECCA, Prince Edward County Christian Association was formed. Many of those that taught in the centers were teachers who did not leave after the school closing. The centers were formed in communities by using churches, other buildings that were available including their homes. Mrs. Flossie Scott White Hudson will tell her story of how she allowed her newly built home to be used to provide children some type of schooling.

Flossie Scott White Hudson

Flossie Scott White Hudson tells me her journey not only as a parent, but one who provided space for children to learn. "In the summer of 1959, when the Board of Supervisors closed all county schools to avoid integration, Mrs. White was concerned that children would not be motivated to study at home.

It was suggested at one of the many meetings being held at First Baptist Church that centers be opened if available space could be found. Mrs. White, a widow, had just moved into her house with a large basement in the fall of 1958, so she volunteered and opened her home to the children in the community. She was a self-employed beautician and could schedule her work for evenings and weekends. The Center opened from September to May, five days a week from 9:00 am to 3:00 pm.

Mrs. White was blessed to have two elderly aunts who were retired teachers to help her, Mrs. Pearl C. Allen and Mrs. D. Althea Jones. They were advised not to call it a school, so it was called the White Recreation Center.

The center was well attended with an average of over 50 students a day. Some families had as many as six children attending the Center.

The subjects were the same as those taught in school using any books that were available. Newspapers were read daily especially the Journal and Guide to know what was happening in court.

A 4-H Club was organized with the help of the Cooperative Extension Service that continued to meet after schools reopened. Mrs. White and Mrs. Jones were 4-H leaders. 4-

H members attended the annual 4-H conference at VPI each year to demonstrate their projects and compete with members from other counties in the state, often winning first and second place. A young girl, Wendy Lyle was inspired to be an exchange student and studied in Spain. A young fella, Lacy Ward Jr., played in the state band and was selected for the National Band that toured Europe that summer.

After the first year the schools were closed, many of the older children were sent away to school, but the basement was still over crowded, so Mrs. Allen and Mrs. Jones opened another center nearby. Mrs. Allen was so dedicated that that she walked a total of six miles daily.

Mrs. White still needed help so she used a fifth-grade student, Lena Mitchell, as her helper.

When school closed, she had one son, he was nine years old. He stayed home the first year, the second year her sister insisted that she let him come to Newport News with her; so, he was in Newport News three years. She lost him when he was 21; he was in a car wreck.

Mrs. White was happy when the Free Schools opened in 1964, but she missed the children she had worked with for four years.

Mrs. White remarried in 1967, and will now be referred to as Mrs. Flossie Hudson.

After the schools reopened, Mrs. Hudson continued to be very active in the community. She served as a 4-H leader for over 25 years and worked closely with the Home Demonstration Club. She was also a member of the NAACP, Voters League, and other clubs in the community.

In 1966, she was employed by the Prince Edward County

community Action Agency as an Outreach Worker. Her job was to visit homes and interview people to determine what was needed in their community. The agency's motto was "Helping people to help themselves". While working as an Outreach Worker, she organized a Senior Citizens Club who founded the Cross Road Senior Citizens Center.

In 1970, when the counties merged, she was employed by Central Piedmont Action Council (C-PAC). She was later placed in the Elderly Nutrition Program where she was promoted to director of the program.

She is an active member of the Sulphur Spring Baptist Church where she has held many offices.

At the age of 94, she still drives herself to the "Y" on Tuesdays and Thursdays, to the Senior Citizens' Centers on Mondays and Wednesdays, and stays at home on Fridays, if there is no other meeting or anything else, she attends.

*Excerpts from **Reverend L. Francis Griffin's** Preface of the Training Centers*

In 1959, the Board of Supervisors of Prince Edward County elected to close public schools. Therefore, approximately 3400 children of both races suddenly found themselves without any form of school. The white citizens proceeded at once to form private schools to aid the 1400 white children involved. As a result of this action, the Southside Schools, Inc. was created, and later received a charter granted by the State Cooperation Commission.

However, the approximately 1700 Negro children were without any form of school. The Negro parents and children of this little Virginia community were reluctant to accept private schools and did not wish to revert to a pre-1954 status found themselves without any plans for the future of their children. In November, the Negro citizens called a mass meeting, and formed the Prince Edward County Christian Association to meet an unprecedented crisis.

L. Francis Griffin
President of P.E.C.C.A.,
and Coordinator of Project 1700

Map of Center's Locations

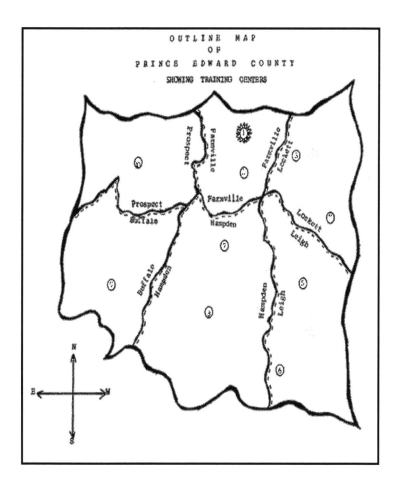

The Choices They Were Forced to Make

Parents were struggling to find a solution for their children to attend school. In addition to that, there were parents of the tar paper shack era, part of the student walkout, participated in boycotting the stores and after work walked with students in the streets protesting. The parents and their children will share their stories.

Mrs. Carrie Jefferson -Yolanda Bigger Gladden's mother

"I was one of the students who were involved in the Historical Student Walkout in 1951 by the Leadership of Barbara Johns.

"When school closed, well I did the best I could. I wasn't working at the time, and we just sent our kids to the schools that were opened at the churches, such as First Baptist Church. At that time, I had two children in school. I remained in Farmville, (Prince Edward County) the whole time, I didn't go out of town, and they just went to the free schools here. We all remained in Prince Edward until the schools reopened. When school reopened the children went to school to continue their education. All my children finished school in Prince Edward County."

YoLanda Bigger - Gladden

I was four years old when school closed, so that would make me at that time preschool. How did I find out about school closing–that part I'm not sure.

Mother probably followed through since she was part of the plaintiff group, to get us to whatever classes and learning that we could go to. I was a baby, so I had no recollection to how I felt when school closed. When school closed, I was still in Prince Edward County area Alternative schools. I know we were taught in the First Baptist Church basement, a lot of our basic educational skills. When to kind of figure out what class to put us in, and I wanted to say they started me probably between fifth and sixth grade. I stayed in school and graduated in 1972 at Prince Edward County High School.

Now I am 60 years old, I recently been retired, I guess you would say or... and I am on disability.

Mary Brown – Carolyn Brown's mother

Mary Brown recalls, "It really affected my life as a parent. It was disappointing and I was hurt and it was really quite a problem for me to begin with, but then God gave me a way to put them in school, so I took my twin girls to school in Philadelphia. They were put with a beautiful family; they worked with them and helped them.

My son was sent to Iowa, he moved with a beautiful white family, they were good to him and one of the boys came back to see him when school opened here. My son finished school in the military. I took them away myself and stayed with them the whole time. I worked and took care of them, they got in the best schools, and they got in good schools. They went to school for two years before we came back home, so school hadn't opened up so the NAACP sent them to Massachusetts to go to school there. When Free School opened here Kitty went to New York and stayed with their sister, Barbara, but Carolyn came back home and finished school here. My son joined the military and finished school in Germany.

I had to make a decision for them not to lose out, I wanted them educated, so I made the decision to take them away to school. That's why I did that because I didn't know how long school was going to stay closed. I think I did really good about people helping me and met beautiful people that gave me help. I'm not sorry I made that decision because they all graduated and made a life for themselves.

I'm grateful they made it. They all graduated. It was hard though, leaving your home not really knowing what would happen to you, but I give all the praise to the Lord, because he made a way for me and I did all right."

Carolyn Brown

I was in the 5th grade when school closed in 1959. I found out about the school closing from my mother. When I heard that school was closed, actually I was glad I didn't have to go to school that year. After school closed, I went to Philadelphia the first two years, my mother moved to Philadelphia and the next or two years I went to Massachusetts; the American Friends sent us there.

When school opened, I was in the 9th grade, enrolled at Robert R. Moton and graduated from Moton. I am retired from Roche Carolina (formerly Hoffman LA Roche) in Jersey. Actually, I think my opportunity was better because it did close. It gave me more options; I don't think I would have. I probably had been a secretary, which was not bad, but I wouldn't have thought that I could do that. I just felt that destiny took me this way and it worked out, I think, I graduated from Moton. I think, better than it would have worked out if I had stayed. You know, by going away to different places, it kind of heighten my horizon letting me know what I could do. And when I graduated from Moton, If I had no opportunity to go away and meet people and be exposed to different things, I think I would have just settled for whatever that came my way.

I don't feel angry about it or I guess during that time, but now I don't feel any.... or anything, because I felt that was the way destiny took me. If I had been one of the people who didn't go anyplace, I might have felt differently. I would have felt different and I understand their feelings, but having the opportunity that I had I am really thankful for it, because I don't think I would be retired and able to do what I .... I wouldn't have done that and you don't know.

I do think that the closing of the schools was a turning point for the south, you know for Farmville, because sometimes if things aren't shaken up in a certain way, they tend to be stagnant and keep going the same way. Sometimes in order to change something has to be broken down in order to change. Actually, during those turbulent times, it changed a whole nature of that town and I don't think it would have changed if something didn't happen, because you know the more you, what they say, for things to change; you have to do something different. And even though it seemed like a really bad thing that happened, actually it was a shaken, a lot of times when things change, some people get lost. It happens, it's for the good of the whole, because it's what happen in the country now, like health care and all of that, it seems bad, but it has to change and change comes hard, changes are not easy and for something to change something has to be destroyed in order for it to change, you know?

Mrs. Ernestine Herndon – Charlotte Herndon's mother

My 3rd grade teacher Mrs. Herndon explains the similarities of her predicament with that of other parents in the community.

"Mr. L.L. Hall, principal, held a meeting in 1959, I was teaching 3rd grade, to let us know that school may close. I didn't pay too much attention to it; I took it as a rumor. I couldn't believe schools would close, but when I did not get my contract in the spring, I knew for sure it was true.

The closing of school impacted me greatly, first as a teacher and as a parent. First as a teacher, I had to decide if I was going to leave home and find a teaching position or was, I just going to work. I was fortunately enough to get a teaching position in Spotsvania County. That was good, but I still had to leave my family, but I knew I had to make a decision whether to stay home and not work or go away and work. As a teacher I had to find a job somewhere, as a parent I had to leave 2 children with my mother if I took a job elsewhere. I didn't see my family every week, most of the time it was like once a month, I came home and I saw my children and my mother and my father. My husband was working away in Washington, DC, so the family was split and that wasn't good for the family and it wasn't good for me either.

I went to Spotsylvania County, and by the way I worked in Spotsylvania for three years. I lived in Fredericksburg, and taught in Spotsylvania, about 15 miles away. This was about 100 miles from where I lived in Prince Edward County. I went alone; the next year I took my daughter with me. The next two years I took my son and daughter with me, so they didn't miss any time out of school and that was a fortunate thing and it was a blessing from the Lord that I didn't have to worry about my children being out of school and missing time out of school.

With the school being closed it was very harsh for me. I was riding with another teacher by the name of Mrs. Alma Smith, the car would break down, but the good thing was about the car breaking down, and God was so good, it broke down when we got to Powhatan and I don't know why it always broke down in Powhatan; but that was God's doing, because we were close to home and my children were with me.

During Christmas holiday we were coming home, the car broke down, we couldn't get a bus. Finally, one bus came along and stopped just long enough to tell us that another bus was coming. The second bus didn't stop, but kept going. Well, he stopped long enough to tell us that. It was raining and sleeting and hailing. We were cold and miserable.

The second bus came along and didn't stop at all, it just passed right by us. Mrs. Smith called her husband and she told him in no uncertain terms that he better get down with a taxi and pick us up, so he came that night. We had left that morning from Spotsvania County about 8:00 and when we got home it was 2:00 in the morning. I went back to Spotsylvania because I didn't know if school would reopen, so I kept my job and worked two weeks. When Free School opened in 1963, I came back for an interview and was hired. My children attended the free school and graduated from R.R. Moton High School.

Charlotte Herndon Womack

When school closed, I was too young to start school. Back then we didn't have kindergarten. I was 5 when school closed. So, I stayed out a year with my grandmother so it didn't affect me as far as starting, when school closed, I had gotten old enough to attend. I found out about school closing when they reopen. At five years old and six years old you did what your parents told you to do I was so young I did not know that there was a school here that I was supposed to be going to, so my first experience of school was when we went to Spotsylvania County in Northern Virginia and I was there for three years. First grade, second grade and third grade and then, I never questioned my mom about school because to me that was not abnormal, that was all I knew. We would close the house down and throughout the year we would open it up as far as utilities as far as Christmas and then we would cut the utilities back on in the summer time. When I heard that school was close, I don't want to say it was negative, but it was uprooting me from what I knew. I was glad to come back home, we could stay in our house, but I would make new friends, because the old friends were in Spotsylvania County.

I was in 4th grade when school reopened, and it felt like it was a new school, I did not know there was other kids that never been to school. I did not know there were kids starting school for the first time, 8, 9 10, 11 years old. When school closed, we went to Spotsylvania County, we lived in Fredericksburg for a couple years, but we always went to Spotsylvania County School. We ended up going there because that was where my mother got a teaching job that is where she taught. I went in 60 and two years later my brother went. I thought about it, my mother, 30 some years old traveling with two kids to go to school.

My grandmother kept both of us for a year while my mother went to Spotsylvania County and then I went and my brother went and I remember we would pack the car up on Thursday night and go to school on that Friday morning. Then as soon as school was out I would come home at least once a month, maybe twice a month and we stayed with my grandmother. And I remember saying to my mama one day, I wish every day was Friday and she said why, and I said so we can go home every day so she said if every day was Friday we would have to go to school every day (laughing). We would get up early, early Monday morning because we would stay here Friday, Saturday and Sunday and go straight to school. My grandmother had what you called a potbellied stove and I remember my mama get up in the morning and wouldn't let us get up until she stroked the fire to get the house warm. I remember those kinds of things, because we would always have oil heat here.

When school reopened, I came back here, I was in the fourth grade to the Free Schools. I think that was the year that Robert Kennedy came. I was excited about him coming because I knew he was the brother of John F. Kennedy. I was sitting on the end of the row of chairs in the auditorium. At the end of his speech he was coming up the aisle shaking people hands who were on the end, and I was getting excited and we had one student in my class that came in late and my teacher made me move one seat over and he got to shake his hand and I was so mad with him. I was at the Elementary school, what they call Branch I. That was the Free Schools.

Now, I am retired after 32 years of teaching in public schools and retired in 09. Some people I've heard said they came back because they felt they wanted to get back to

Prince Edward, I didn't feel like that until later. I came back because it was home.

I am the first generation of girls who wore pants to school. I was in the seventh grade, we walked to school every day.

Mrs. Lillian Jordan-Johnson was 102 years old when I received her written response. Through her daughter, I was able to get this unforgettable memory of the school closing that was left with her and summarized in this one sentence.

Mrs. Libby Jordan (Lillian Jordan-Johnson's mother)

"Sending my children away for schooling was not what we wanted to do, but we had no choice."

Lillian Jordan Johnson

We, my twin sister and I, were just finishing the 8th grade going into the 9th grade when school closed in 1959. I found out about the school closing really from my parents, mom and daddy because my sister and I lived a very sheltered life and mommy and daddy didn't talk about things to us and we didn't even realize what was going on particularly after school closed. We had an aunt from New York that had come down and we hadn't seen her for, really for years, I don't think I had ever seen her and she went back to New York and after that momma and daddy were packing up me and my sister Phyllis to go to New York to live with my aunt. I remember my momma was very sad, momma was very upset, she said I got to send my babies away, but they knew that it was only God to had my aunt to come down for a visit and she said that she would take us up there and stay with her.

We were just green as grass, we didn't know anything and momma and daddy didn't talk about things like that, so we didn't really know what was all going on. We heard them talking about the school closing, I think we heard more about it when we got to New York, because when we got to New York with my aunt; she lived in the Bronx, we were not two blocks from the school and when we started going to the school and when the teachers found out where we were from they just wanted us to tell them, talk about what happened and so they just wanted us to tell about it, because they knew about it, they heard it on the news and everything and we would hear momma tell us about what would happen with the court proceedings when we go back at holidays and in the summertime and we would hear about it.

Like I said we were very spoiled and sheltered, so a lot of the negative stuff we didn't hear about it and then we began when we were there in school, different ones would tell us about it and we would hear about it. We stayed with that aunt about a year and a half in New York and my aunt died. Her husband remarried and my daddy brought us back down here. A lady, Ms. Jeffries in Charlotte County wanted to help some of the children over here, so she took us that January to stay with her and her family in Charlotte County to go to the schools over there. We went back and forth to Charlotte County; we were now in the 11th grade. And then that lady got sick and she couldn't take care of us anymore, because she really had five kids of her own.

During our last year daddy wanted us to graduate some way, so they would take us 30 miles over to the bus to the Appomattox line. Right at Appomattox line there was a bus that would take you over to Charlotte County to the school, but it was people turning in people and reporting us. It wasn't white people; it was black people. They began to say that it was too many kids standing there at that bus stop, because other children were standing there too. That was like the meeting place, so what momma or daddy did, they would get up every morning and drive us over to the Charlotte line to a house over there to some people we had come to know and there we would take the bus. There was, I think two other kids too. That would be the first bus for the Charlotte County High School. Mama and daddy did all of that to make the sacrifice so we could graduate; they did that the whole year, the whole trip was about 30 miles one way and they would take us over there and the bus would bring us back every day to that house and mamma and daddy would take us home and every morning they would bring us back. We did that until we graduated in June in 1963 at Central High School in Charlotte County.

After we graduated, we went to Hampton Institute and graduated. My sister Phyllis taught that year at the high school of Prince Edward County Public schools and went to Texas. She retired from school in Georgia. I went to Hampton one year and went to New York around 1964, 1965 and got married and start having kids and lived there for 40 some years.

I really felt bad for my friends, some of them didn't have family and friend to go away to, some of the boys went to work, even though the Quakers, because mama worked with the Quakers, she would be with some of them that would take the kids in the church and teach them from the magazines. Mama was in the Ebony magazine teaching them from the magazines. She is still living and she is 102, on March 30th next year if the Lord is willing, she will be one-hundred-and three (103).

They weren't allowed to use books, so they would teach the children that couldn't go away from magazines, I think they couldn't say it was a school and if they used books, they would try to classify it as a school. After you figure all that time a lot of them didn't go back, I really felt bad for them that they missed out, even though things worked out for them, those that went back to school, they tried to bring them to the grade they were in. You know if you are 19 or 20, you don't want to go back to the grade, so they tried to help them out, so I felt bad for those who were not fortunate like we were to take them in, but thank God, it all worked out. I discovered back during that time too, it was a lot of white kids was suffering along with us, because they didn't have any place to go either and they couldn't afford to go to the private school.

I am retired and a licensed and ordained minister. I am called an evangelist.

Mrs. Hazel Miser - Shirley Eanes' mother

Hazel Miser was another parent, and one of the students who were involved in the 1951 strike; she was eager to tell her story.

I was one of the 1951 strikers of the historical walkout in Prince Edward County. The school closing impacted my life as a parent, taking the time out to teach my children. My oldest Shirley and the other three I didn't have to teach them because everything I taught her, they learned.

I didn't have to make any special arrangements other than to teach my kids. I did a lot of sewing and making quilts. While school was closed, they went to free school in Prospect, Virginia at the Methodist Church until the regular school opened. When the school opened in Prince Edward County, I sent all of them to school and I went to work.

Shirley Ann Davison - Eanes

When school closed in 1959, I wasn't in any grade. I was 6 years old. I was old enough to go to school but I had not started. I didn't find about the school closing until several years later after they closed. My mother never told me why I wasn't going to school. She just said that you are not going to school yet. When I heard that school had closed, if I remember correctly I think I probably felt like it was something that I had done; the reason schools had closed stems from something else that was going on in my personal life. I think I associated everything that happened outside my home environment, and kind of put it all together and made it part of my home environment. So if the schools were not operating, it had something to do with my home environment. I didn't have a lot of contact with the outside world other than my home environment and people that came into my home environment. When school closed, I did not go to any schools. I did not go to any public schools or private schools. As I said before, everything centered around my home environment, my mother taught me at home after a year or so, probably around age seven or maybe she started at age six. I am not real sure what age she started, however my earliest remembrance of being taught anything was at home. And that was learning the alphabets and having my mother read to us all the time.

When school reopened, just prior to 1963, I do remember going to a couple of centers, I remember being at a center here in Farmville at the First Baptist Church and the

Methodist Church. I remember having classes between the two places. I remember going across the street to go to First Baptist and then crossing the street going back to the African Methodist church. I remember going to the Miller Dentist office building doing something in the basement and I also remember at one time I went to the Methodist Church in Prospect. I remembered that any of those centers I never stayed there any more than a day or two, maybe three. The longest time I was at one of them was down town at First Baptist. I think it was a weeklong thing or three or four days at the end of whatever we were doing.

We put on a play and that was my first time singing publicly. I had a singing part in a Tom Sawyer play in that church. I don't remember learning very much there, I don't remember being taught alphabets or how to read, I don't remember being taught any math. I knew how to read and math. The only skills that I learned; my mother taught me. She was not a teacher, matter of fact my mother was a 1951 walk out student here at Moton High School at that particular time. She was 16 and she was in the 11th grade at the time of the strike. When school reopened, I wasn't in a grade because I never went to school. I ended up in the 5th grade, and when I say I ended up in the 5th grade because I remember one day being in the 3rd grade, I remember another day being in the 4th grade and then I finally was in the 5th grade for the four years. I attended the Mary E. Branch Elementary School, #2, which is the former Moton High School. I finished school at Prince Edward County High School. The year before I graduated, they changed the name of the school. They changed it from R.R. Moton High School to Prince Edward County High School. That was my junior year and I was about to order my class ring, and I was very upset, because I wanted Moton on my ring.

Now, I am semi-retired and I work here at the Moton

Museum since July 23, 2013 and July 23, 2014, it will be a year for me here.

Gladys Julliet Rainey-Cathy Allen-Williams mother

Gladys Julliet Rainey remembers vividly her experience as a parent of the school closing.

Oh, my Lord, I hardly don't know what to say on how the school closing affected my life as a parent. It was just the more dreadful thing that I think would ever happen in Prince Edward. I never thought that anything like that would happen. I just think what a hard thing it would have on myself and my children. And I am so thankful that at the time they had a father that was a teacher and that was a help to them. The decision to close the school forced me to make some choices. I didn't have to move, the children being so young. I had a son that was old enough to go to school, so we just did the best with him, staying at home with the help of his father. We made out until things got better. I didn't have to make any special arrangements.

When school reopened in Prince Edward County, the first thing I said was thank you Lord. That gave me a chance at knowing my children will be back in school. And that was about the biggest and blessed thing that could have happened, them back in school and I know they had a place to go and not be sent away from home, because I love my children so well that I always want them to be at home, so when school reopened that helped me because I didn't know if I was going to have to make some other decision to send them somewhere. I just want to thank the Lord for it.

You know it's hard to think that you would ever witness something like that. After all of these years of living in Prince Edward, I thought that they would never do something like that, make so many changes. It wasn't just hard on the children; it was hard on the parents too. So, we just have so much to be thankful for that things did work out. Things are not where we would like for it to be, but we hope and pray that things will continue to get better. I remember when they boycotted the stores, oh yea; they ran from one place to another. I think that was about the worst thing. I had to go to different places because I wasn't satisfied. We had to go grocery shopping.

At that time people didn't have transportation like they have today, so they had to hire somebody to take them to this place or another. It was a time for everybody. I was blessed that I had transportation, because a lot of people didn't have transportation to go from one place to another, leave Prince Edward to go to Lynchburg, Crewe or Blackstone. We thank the Lord that everything happened in our behalf and we hope that things continue.

Cathy Allen-Williams

I was three-years old when school closed in 1959. When I realized and I found out about school closing, you heard your parents and everyone talking about it. Of course, I was upset because everyone wanted to go to school and learn. We had school at our church at High Rock Baptist Church. Some families that had older children had to send them to relatives, or other counties to go to school, but that part didn't really affect me.

When school reopened, I went to Mary E. Branch I and I

was in the 3rd. grade. After 3rd grade, for 4th grade I went to Worsham Elementary School. After Worsham, our family moved to Rhode Island, I spent 1 year in Rhode Island 5th grade, and for 6th grade I came back to Rice Elementary school and 7th through 12th. I attended Prince Edward County School and graduated in 1975.

Now I am employed with the U.S. Postal service. If school had not closed, I probably wanted to be a singer, because I am still doing that, but not on a level I would like to be. I hope that people will learn from their mistakes and won't repeat what happened years ago.

Helen R. Walker – Angeline Holliman Gee's mother

Instead of sending her five children away, Helen had to think of an alternative plan for providing her children with some type of education. She chose to homeschool them. She tells how the school closing affected her life.

As a parent the school affected my life. I felt that I was shocked, dumb founded, wondering what I was going to do, how I was going to do it and what I was going to do to get started because it seemed like closing of the school was the worst thing that could have happened because the children are at home, they are not learning anything so I just got my little stuff together the first year, my oldest son was starting school, he was six years old and it was just unthinkable that he wasn't able to go to school.

The decision of the closing of the school forced me to make-I had to make a decision about how my children were going to get an education and the decision that I made was to find some kind of school supplies and to come home and teach him what I knew myself.

I had to make quite a few arrangements because things were difficult at that time, because my husband at that time was working on the Northern Western Railroad, he was gone most of the times, he was only there on the weekends. So after I sit down and pondered for a while, I said I got to do something, so I made a decision and I took a retired school teacher, her name was Ms. Beatrice Lawson Davenport and I talked to her and she agreed to come. We lived in Prospect, Virginia and she lived in Tuggle Virginia, so I agreed to pick her up after she agreed to come and bring her here and would take her back home when she finished, but she wouldn't take any pay at all. And then I bought this Bible, a colorful Bible, so I could read to the children because to me the most important thing to me was reading.

When the Free school opened in Prince Edward County, I got them children out the bed, comb their heads, it was just so after all this time, it was just amazing to get up with a purpose, go to school, yaw going to school today (laughing).

Angeline Gee -Holliman

 I was not old enough to go to school when school closed. I was 4 years old. We use to go to school in the bottom of Saint James Church in Prospect, Virginia. When the free school opened Ghee was helping and Freddie Cobbs was there helping the children. At that time mama or daddy would bring us to the school and sometime they would come together to pick me up. We also had a lady to come into the

house, Mrs. Beatrice Davenport to teach us. At that time daddy went to talk to her about tutoring us in the house and she agreed to it. Mama went down to the Rexall store and she bought books and things for us to get us started, and Ms. Davenport made a big chart with the time tables on it and all of the numbers and everything, that is how we learned at home. It started at home and then we went to Saint James. Then we went to go to school in the bottom of Saint James Church in Prospect, where I lived. I was 6 or 7. A lot of learning was from mom, because she taught us how to read. I was 8 years old when school reopened.

Ruth Watkins

Ruth Watkins tells her account. She is the mother of Delores, Mary and Hope. "School closing did not have too much effect on me as a parent because I was working in another county and I was able to take my children with me. The closing of the schools forced me to make a schedule of what I needed to do because taking the children with me caused for more work than just going myself because I had to do more things at night to be ready to have them ready to ride with me and to be sure that everybody had everything they needed at the right time. When Free School opened in Prince Edward County, I withdrew them from Appomattox and re-enrolled them in Prince Edward. All four of them continued their education in Prince Edward and all four of them graduated from high school in Prince Edward.

Delores Watkins Scott

I was 6 years old when school closed. I found out about the school closing when my mother told me. When I heard about the school closing, I guess at 6, I didn't really think about what it or what the impact meant.

When school closed, my mother taught in Appomattox County, and she took us to school in Appomattox. When school reopened, I came back to Prince Edward and started school here. I went up to the fourth grade in Appomattox, so when I got back here, I was skipped a grade, probably because I had been in school and other kids hadn't and I was a little more advanced I assumed. I finished school at Prince Edward, it was still Robert R. Moton High School when I finished.

I am now a Dean of Students at a Community College in Virginia. Because I was privileged and able to go to school, I think I am doing what I would have wanted to do and I think because I was able to go for those four years there was an impact, but a different impact.

I think, one of the things that I often say to people that fair is not equal and equal is not fair, and that what I believe I learned from the closing of the schools in that we so often think about we want to be fair to everybody and fair is just not the same thing for everybody and equal isn't the same thing for everybody. So, that's something I kind of took away.

Mary Louise Watkins Pace

When the school closed, I was not in school, I would have entered school the following year. Well, I found out about the school closing when it was time for me to go to school, I realized that I could not go to school in Prince Edward County, that I had to go to school elsewhere. I started school in Appomattox County Public Schools. My mother was teaching in Appomattox and that was one of the fortunate things for us, there was four of us. She was teaching there and we were able to go to school with her. I had an older sister and brother, needless to say, they went long before I did, but I did go three years and I had a younger sister who went there two years. I went there for first grade, second grade and third grade. At the end of third grade I came back to Prince Edward County as a fourth-grade student and that was the year that the Free Schools reopened. Once I came back to Prince Edward County as a fourth-grade student, I stayed here until I graduated from high school.

Now, I am retired from the San Antonia, school district in Texas as a teacher and again my second retirement from Richmond schools, I retired as a school administrator. I was assistant principal at an elementary school. Aside from the school closing being a tragic event, more tragic for them than for me. I think that it didn't have to happen and it has affected the country and many generations. And I say that meaning it made a negative impact on the community. The community suffered. I think we lost many, many students, many students who could have done great things, but they were unable to do because they did not have the opportunity to go to school. There were some families of course that were fortunately enough to have somewhere to send their children, but those that didn't the students suffered, the students stayed at home and with the student staying at home, well you know, I often think about them being there, their parents had limited skills, they didn't have skills to pass on to the students and we just lost a lot, they went to school, they did learn, but by the time that many of them got to school, they were four years behind already, and when they came out of school, they were at an age that they needed to go to work and college was unforeseen in their lives, so we lost several generations with that.

Hope Watkins Sutton Justice

 When school closed, I was not old enough to go, I was 4 years old. When I was older, it was a known fact, by my parents and grandparents. Actually, to hear and understand it, was when I was in the 1st grade and I was amazed that people would go to that extent to close schools.

After school closed, I went to Appomattox County School in Appomattox, Virginia when I entered the first grade.

When schools reopened in Prince Edward County, I left Appomattox County and entered school in Prince Edward County. When I came back here, I entered Mary E. Branch number 1. I completed school here; I graduated in 1973 from Robert R. Moton High School.

Now I am an educator. I teach the nurse aide program for Prince George County at Rowanty Technical Center in Carson, Virginia.

School closing still amazes me that people would go to the extent of closing schools and denying education to everyone because of race or because of your skin color. I am still amazed by it and today I still see effects of it, I still see the uh, I still see the principle or desegregation or the prejudices. It's still very obvious to me that it still exists and I am amazed, I am amazed that people do that, close the schools that are into so much segregation. It still amazes me.

Eloise Lockett Jordan

Eloise Lockett Jordan gives a sense of how it was to wait for school to reopen with two young children.

I had two school aged children and we had to figure out how and where we were going to send them to school. One of my sons was 8 and the other one was 6. Our only option initially was to send them to a training school in a basement of the Methodist church in Prospect, Virginia.

There was no decision to make. We could not afford to move to another county and we were not sending our kids away to live with strangers or relatives in other counties. Therefore, our only option was the training school.

We waited for two years for the schools to open and nothing happened. My parents decided to try to get the children into Appomattox County schools. To do this they established a fake residence at an old house in Appomattox. We transported the children to that house daily until my parents were able to move. We never moved to Appomattox so we enrolled our sons in Prince Edward schools. Both my sons were placed in higher grades and my oldest son graduated high school at 17 years old. My other son graduated three years later.

Willie Morton

 *Willie Morton graciously gave me the story of him and his boys while sitting outside under a huge tent on a hot August sunny day. This was the day he was enjoying his family/community gathering, a tradition that started in 1848 and has been celebrated each year for 171 years.* "Living in Prince Edward, my oldest son started school the year school closed. I had to take him to Keysville to

Charlotte County to live with his grandmother to go to school down there for a while. He got sick while he was down there and that didn't work out too good. After he got sick his grandma couldn't handle him and the works, she was old too, and we had to bring him back home and it was terrible, it was a lost year for him, so he lost one year in school.

When school reopened, my second boy started school at that time. Since he was young at that age it didn't affect him that much, but it did throw the two boys back 1 year. They finished school at Prince Edward. Thanks be to God, they were only one year behind. They graduated from Prince Edward County High School.

How do I feel about the school closing? Well, naturally I can't express the words the way I feel, but it was a tragedy type of thing closing schools. Anytime anybody closes things that give any education, any type of schooling and, any time somebody closes something like that I feel like it's a bad thing to do. As far as my kids were concerned, I am kind of glad that they were real young and just starting, but it hurts, not only my kids, it hurts me to see the other kids that are in the community suffer, some leaving home and can't come back, some having to go to school other places, some didn't even get to go to school, it is a hard thing to think about.

Frances Goldman Scott

Frances Goldman Scott was a parent who lived in two Prince Edward school eras. She was not only a parent of a child during the school closing, but she was one of the children who lived through the tar papered shack era.

I attended school in the tar papered building at Robert R. Moton High School. I am the parent of one son, Willie LaGrant Scott, who was affected by the closing of the schools at that time. As a parent the closing of the schools affected me greatly, because not only did I have LaGrant in school, but my oldest daughter. When they closed the school was the day for her to start, and then I had three other children, so it was quite a deal when the schools closed.

We stayed here in Prince Edward County and I drove to Ashton, Virginia every other week to pick him up, bring him home and took him back Sunday. Ashton was 14 miles from Richmond, Virginia, yea, I did that. Because my husband worked, he worked Sundays, maybe every other Sunday or something like that. He didn't have the time to do it, so I did it. And one year we had another student from here that rode with us. My son stayed with a minister and his wife; their last names were Andrews. They did so much for him, they said he was a nice child and he did so well. Usually children get homesick, but he stood the test. Yea, did well in school and I was happy about that. He graduated from Prince Edward County High School. The name had changed from Robert R. Moton High School.

In recalling some of the things we went through with the school closing, I can remember my husband took it very hard when we had to send our son away and that made me, I had to be strong, not only for him, but for the children too seeing their dad upset over this, and there are a lot of other times when I had to do things, go to meetings and all and to insure myself and others that we were going to get through this. And so, I just like to say that you know these were trying times.

Sally Ward

Sally Ward tells her story of two journeys; both as a parent and as one who participated in boycotting the local grocery stores. Her detailed recollection includes her husband, the NAACP and Community Leader Reverend Francis L. Griffin. "The school closing impacted my life as a parent by the kids couldn't go to school. It hurt me real bad because the kids couldn't go to school, And they wanted to know why they couldn't go and the only answer I could come up with was that the color of their skin. It hurt me re-a-l bad, just I still can't get over it up until now. I still can't, because the kids could have gone a long way, I could imagine because Curtis and Pat went back, but they were about 6 or 7 years old in the first grade and that was a great impact on me too.

I had to do a lot of, lot of thinking just what to do, and I didn't have anybody away I could send them to but my brother, he lived in Philadelphia, but at that time he didn't have things prepared for me to send them there, so they didn't go anywhere, they just stayed around the house, I didn't send them anywhere. They use to go down to First Baptist Church part of the day (where they had a makeshift school in the church basement) and the rest of the day they didn't have anything else to do. I sent them down there every day from morning until noon; they stayed down at First Baptist Church. That is the only thing I could do; I didn't know anything I could do at that time. They played, they cried, they carried on some kind of bad because they like school. And Curtis carried on, why they hate us so bad, mama why we can't go to school? And that upset me because I couldn't halfway work and then my husband Burnell, he got all upset about it, we were just shocked in this little town the people hate so much, the little kids.

When Free School opened in Prince Edward County, I

enrolled them in there and they went every day. I was hoping that they would continue with it, but it didn't last but a year, so they stayed out of school until they got them opened. We worked every day, my husband worked one job, I worked another. I used to be so tired, we would come to town and meet at the First Baptist Church and we marched, and we marched, and we marched and we marched every single day, from 1959 to 1964. Then Reverend Griffin told us, the only power a poor person have is your pocketbook, it's power and he told us to stop shopping in the stores and on Saturday we use to meet in front of First Baptist Church and we all were in a line walking across the bridge over to Cumberland County to Osborne Store and Ayers Building Supply.

All you could see is a line of us going to get our little groceries. The NAACP had wheels to come pick us up with our groceries. We boycotted the stores for about three years; we made Farmville a ghost town, that's how I know who spends the money. They told us to go in the store, just go in the store, a whole pile of us, but don't buy anything. They were standing there waiting for us to buy, but we would not buy, we stuck together. One little black man from somewhere, he had come out there with his little bag and got half way through the shopping center and we made a big circle around him, and we said Uncle Tom, Uncle Tom and he fell down, lost his little bag and all his stuff fell on the ground, I will never forget it. The town had big trucks, all you could see was rotten meat, rotten food, we were the ones that bought all of that stuff, I learned a lot, then Martin Luther King came to the church and he told us no violence, no violence and that went on for the longest. Henry Marsh, Governor Doug Wilder and another man, because they locked up one man, I can't think of the one they locked up came up here and there was some little black children was sitting on First Baptist Church courthouse and the police caught them by the arms, dragged them and threw them in jail. I put a big article in the Farmville Herald about the school closing and they had Sam Williams talking about it and I called him and told him, that you all were not around here, we were the foot soldiers that walked every day my husband and I walked from Virginia Street, worked, walked back to the streets to be there at the courthouse with the kids and every night

Reverend Griffin said if they ever get us back down there again, ain't no more coming back and he said if you vote for a person in office and they don't do right the first time, don't vote for them again, that's what he said about one of our own.

Reverend Griffin was one of the finest men, he didn't care who you were, a drunk, homeless, anybody, he always stopped to talk and they asked him was he afraid to walk the streets at night and he said no, I'm not afraid.

Note: Throughout this book you will hear many talk about the Free School. The Free school to some were the Centers provided throughout the counties after school closed. The providers were not allowed to call them schools, but some understood it to be just that. It was confusing because the centers provided practically the same curriculum as the public school. The actual Free School did not occur until the year school re-opened in 1964.

CHILDREN OF MASSIVE RESISTANCE

Stories You Will Hear

After eight years of court cases and delays related to school desegregation, the Prince County Board of Supervisors votes not to fund public schools in the 1959 - 1960 school year. Meantime there were children not old enough to go to school, waiting for that day. When that day came school was closed, therefore they were adversely affected by this decision. Here are their stories:

Willie Edward Clark, Jr.

I had just started in the first grade when school closed in Prince Edward. Just started- six years old. I found out that school had closed through my parents and through the news. I was ripping and rearing and ready to go to school every day and just one day they just said we weren't going to school anymore. So, you know, I couldn't go, just couldn't go. When I heard it, I felt - I felt bad because I just started in school and you know that's something you want to do, - when you hear about – I'm getting ready to start school, I am getting ready to go to school, you ripping and rearing, ready to go, and then to have it just cut off all of a sudden like that it's – it's something.

When school closed, we went to our parent's kin people in Cumberland, so we moved across the bridge, right across Cumberland Bridge and stayed with our cousins over there to go to public school, which was just a little two room school. When school reopened, we came back to Prince Edward, we enrolled back in school. I went and finished school here, graduated from Robert R. Moton. It was

Robert R. Moton at the time. I graduated in 1969, I took two grades in one year, the 11th and 12th grade in one year to graduate on time. I didn't play any sports like I wanted to though, I guess the education meant more than playing sports.

If school had not closed, I guess - I know I would continue and finish. I would have liked to have gone to college, but by the time all of this happen and we came back to Prince Edward my mother, she was stricken down with arthritis, and we just couldn't do what we wanted to do then because we had to stay there take care of her most of the time after school and come back and do what we had to do for her and that just, I mean I don't regret it or anything because that's my mother and I had to do what I had to do to help her.

I'm working for the department of corrections, I've been working for them for 30, almost 33 years. I worked a little while for the Craddock Terry Shoe Factory, and I worked a little while when they had Uniroyal factory and I worked in construction for a little while, all were in Prince Edward. Then after all that I went into corrections, I've been into corrections for 33 years and I am almost ready to retire (laughing)– in 26 more days I will be retiring, 26 more days and I am counting down.

Well what I really would like to add is that I wish it hadn't closed, and I wished everyone could have come to some agreement so, everybody could have graduated together and on time, that is what I really wished, but you know (paused) it happened, so we couldn't do anything about it, so we did graduated, most of us. I guess it was a setback for us but we survived, we have survived and we are still surviving.

Reverend Leon Jackson

 Actually, when school closed, I had never started school, I was not old enough to go to school, I was born in 1954. When school was closed I turned nine years old, I attended school for the first time at nine years old. I found out about the school closing by parents, relatives and friends. When I heard about the school closing...well, I felt depressed, because for some reason everybody wants to start school and I wanted to start school and didn't have a school to go to, so what they did was, I remember going to Levi Church. They had a little building there in Meherrin, Virginia and we went up there and spent a half a day, trying to teach us little things. I never will forget it because we didn't have much transportation and they use to drop us off and sometimes we would have to walk back, that was about five or six miles. Yea, it was fun because it was a bunch of us together.

When school opened, we were excited, I remember going to Mary E. Branch II, which is the Moton Museum now, we went there first, our parents took us and we got some shots of all kinds of paperwork done, and I remember the school bus was sitting there, and we went up on it. I had never been on a school bus before, I thought it was exciting, yea, I was really excited about it to go to school, but when we went to school, I was kind of depressed because everybody there was in one classroom, it was to the max, my cousins and nephews and whatever, they were seven, eight years older than I was. Something just didn't seem right, but the first two days, we didn't do anything, they just tried to group you and then and it took a while, my brother was in the class with me, he had a mental situation and I knew he wasn't supposed to be in there, nobody knew, the teachers didn't know. A long time he stayed until they found it out, and finally they put him where he should have.

I stayed in school and I had some great teachers, principals that were concerned. I remember Ms. Vera Allen, Mrs. Herndon; all those teachers really cared about you. I can't see how they did it, because it was a lot of us. They made sure that we got what we needed, they took the time, and after I got in high school and middle school, I couldn't see how one teacher could take the time with 32 children. They made a difference in my life. Mrs. Herndon made you feel like she was your mom. I was the youngest out of 12 children to finish high school. I think if I had a fair share of education, I would have been much more, but my spelling was never really that great, did pretty good on math, I think I could have done much better than I am, but I thank them for where I am and strived to get there. I graduated from Prince Edward County High school in 1974.

Now here is the thing, I was behind in school the whole school turn, when I got to the tenth, I think it was the 11th, they doubled up on my history, government and science. Ms. Rawlins, she made a difference too, but I had to take two English and catch up, so I could graduate at least at nineteen. I graduated at 19, an old man (laughing).

Once I graduated from high school, I stayed with the school system and continued to drive the school bus, for some reason, I love driving the school bus, you got more when you graduated. I drove the school bus and then I worked in the cafeteria. I worked as custodian at night so I had three jobs all at Prince Edward. When I graduated from high school it was just like graduating from college, I was the first in my family that did it, I remember that night plain as day at Longwood College, my family just stood up and cheered and cheered, and cheered (laughing), they felt so proud (continued laughing).

Harry Lee Eddins, Jr.

 I wasn't in school when school closed in 1959. I was born in 56, I was like three years old. When I was old enough to go to school, it was a lot of protesting at that time. My sister who is a year older than I went to school at First Baptist Church and the AME (African Methodist Episcopal). I was too young to understand the concept of school closed, but I used to live off of the avenues, which is first, second, third Avenue and we used to come through there to go to the store, and we used to see white kids go to school and they seem to be having fun. When school reopened, I had a little animosity against white people because I didn't think the school books were fair to our history. They left out a lot of our history concerning the country in our studies, so our books were half-truths.

When school opened, we went back to Branch I and Branch II and when I was old enough to go to high school, it was R.R. Moton, which they later named it Prince Edward High School. I completed high school, it turned into Prince Edward when I was in school, well after integration they wanted the white students to come into the school system, so they asked our class to vote to have the name changed. They did. When I went in it was R. R. Moton and I think the principal was Mr. Penn. I think the school board wanted to change it, because – we only had maybe four Caucasian, white kids at school, they were only there because their parents were superintendent kids or something like that or they couldn't afford the private school.

If school had not closed, it made me kind of prejudice

because I seen how much society looked down on us as people of color, and how we had to take a back seat or be second-class citizens. It's kind of harden me, but, as time goes, you get to see all are not prejudice, it was just a few. Farmville as a whole, the closing of the schools was part of it, but the integration, I think we lost in segregation, I think we lost because what was once a thriving black community is lost and we were just pushed to the side.

Joyce Randall Reid

I was in the fourth grade when school closed. I found out about the school closing through the teachers and the principal. I think it was very sad. We were young, but we were sad, we were very sad.

After school closed, we had been out of school about 2 years when my mom took me to New Jersey. We went to New Jersey for a year, a riot broke out, mom and dad brought us back to Farmville and then I went to stay with Ms. Annie Mae Griggs for a while. We went to school in the basement of First Baptist Church. Ms. Annie Mae Griggs was my Godmother. I was about 12 or 13. When school reopened, I went into Branch 2 and then to the high school. I stopped high school in 1969.

I am married and live in Morristown, New Jersey. I am a certified home health aide and I take care of the sick.

Willie Gene Miller

I was five years old when school closed. I was not old enough to go to school when it closed. I found out about the school closing because my aunts and uncles were going to school. I am not sure how I felt when I heard that school was closed; I was a young boy then.

When school closed, I went to school at First Baptist Church and then I went to New York. When school reopened, I moved back to Farmville and began school here at the Elementary School. I graduated at R.R. Moton High School.

I am now retired from construction.

If school hadn't closed, I would have loved to have been here in Farmville. The school closing put a big hurt on Farmville, slowed us down a whole lot, put us back a whole lot. We missed a lot when the school was closed.

Peggy Eddins

 I was not old enough to go to school when school closed. I was four years old. I found out about the school closing by my mother, at the time my brother and I was staying with my great grandmother and my great grandfather on what they call now First Avenue and Second Avenue. We were so young; we didn't think about it when school was closed. Before then we were on a farm and did chores around the house. I didn't think about the school being closed until we came to live with my grandmother and grandfather and Joe Griggs. That was about the time we did start going to school. You see, by us having never gone, it didn't really faze us. We didn't' go anywhere, we stayed between the two-grand mama's while my mother worked and did whatever we could at home, like children … we just did stuff at home. My brother and I were born here, then we moved to Philadelphia and stayed for some years and came back here and that is when we stayed with our two grandparents.

When school reopened, both of us went to Branch I and we

were both put in the right grade. I think it was like the 3rd grade and Bubble was put in the right grade, so really, we both graduated on time. I graduated from Prince Edward County High School in 1973. I went to Keysville twice two different years and took up Career Development. Then I got my certificate for CNA and I got my license and worked at quite a few jobs. I worked in private sitting and Longwood. I left Longwood and went into CNA and now I am disabled.

The school closing didn't really affect me that much when I went into school. It didn't hold us back. I think I was put in the 3rd grade, because I know I graduated in the right year. I did well. When I left Branch 1, I went there until I was in the 6th grade and I was supposed to go to the high school, but they were overcrowded, so we had to end up going Worsham School, 5 miles outside of Farmville. I think it was for half a of year. After they got things situated, we went to high school. I started at R.R. Moton for maybe two years, but when I graduated the name had been changed to Prince Edward County High School. Because I remember when the first white student came to the high school, Patricia Tooa.

Edith L. Goode

When school closed, I was not old enough to go to school. I found out about the school closing from my grandparents. I was only 3 years old. I did not have a reaction. I started school at the age of 4 in Appomattox County because my aunt, uncle and cousins were going there. My parents moved to Maryland and left me with my grandparents while they worked. My grandfather worked on the railroad and my grandmother was a cook. When school re-opened, I stayed in Appomattox schools. I was in the 2nd grade.

James Phillip Goode

I was not yet school age when school closed. I found out about the school closing by my grandparents. I think I was too young to have a reaction. Didn't know why. I just remember seeing the older children not going to school.

I did not go anywhere until it was time for me to enter school two years after the schools closed. I went to Appomattox County Schools.

My dad worked for the railroad and my mother stayed home. My sister and I stayed with my grandparents most of the time. When school re-opened, I stayed in Appomattox County. I was in the 3rd grade.

Now I am retired from the Norfolk and Western Railroad after 30 years of employment. Also spent 4 years in the U.S. Army.

My education was not interrupted because of the school closing, but I always wanted to play football for Prince Edward. Instead of playing on a team with my childhood family and friends, I had to play against them.

Gloria Allen- Lockett

I was not in school at the time when school closed; I was two years of age when the school did close. How did you find out about it- I was so young, I didn't even pay it any attention, I was not aware of it. I didn't have a reaction really; if I did, I can't remember it.

When school was closed, I was at home and played with my siblings at home with my mom and dad. I attended school when it did open at Prince Edward County Branch #1. I continued through school, but I did stop school and I believe it was the 9th or 10th grade. I got my GED, that's what I did.

What I am doing now is I work for a nonprofit organization called the CDIS Head Start Program. I have been with Head Start for a total of 35-plus years and I am still with them and I love it.

For some people you know, it was pretty devastating, but for me it wasn't because of my age and I didn't know any better, so I really can't say. I did miss two years, I only missed two years of school and that was the way I qualified to receive the scholarship, because of the fact that I went to school at age 7 instead of age 5. The scholarship that I received was the Brown v the Board of Education Scholarship. I got my Bachelor Degree and also my Master Degree through that scholarship. This scholarship allowed me the opportunity to work in a field that I have always been interested in working. I do some counseling part time and my title is, I am a qualified Mental Health Provider and I work with families who are in need of mental health skill building services.

Robert Jones

When school closed, I was 4 years old. I heard about the school closing by talk in the community. When I heard about the school closing, I didn't totally understand. When school closed, I stayed at home. Nothing could be done. My mom worked in a white man's kitchen to earn a living and my dad worked at Buffalo Shook and Company in Farmville as a saw miller. When school reopened, I started in 3rd grade, was promoted after 3rd (9 years old), testing.

The five years of school closing set a lot of students back socially, emotionally, psychologically as well as spiritually. Personally, I was bitter, (very bitter) due to the schools closing. I am blessed to have had two wonderful hard-working parents who wanted to see their children become something better than the two of them. Devout Christian parents they never taught their 2 children to hate. My mother Carrie Edwards Jones did most of the talking. my daddy, James M. Jones, Sr. was very quiet but a stern disciplinarian, and he believed each year that schools would reopen.

As rumors spread, they didn't open until five years had passed. Mom did not believe schools would reopen and she was correct. We had cousins in Appomattox County Virginia who were willing to take us in to live during school sessions so that we would not miss school. My mom was 110% in favor but dad wouldn't bulge, internally I was livid because I always loved school. Of course, I couldn't allow my dad to see my displeasure. These were the old days, children weren't allowed to do such, may have gotten a few loose teeth early in life.

I am retired from the Department of Justice/Federal Law Enforcement. If school had not closed, I would like to have been an actor.

As a young child, I became very disturbed about the schools closing in Prince Edward County, Virginia. Each year that schools remained closed I became more angry. I always loved school. The closing never seemed to bother my brother because he never liked attending school much anyway. My mother would often say that there were selfish and mean white people just like there were selfish and mean" coloreds" (that was the adjective used to described black people back then, at least one of quite a few). I read my brother's books more than he would read them. I always love reading and today I still do.

It took years for me to wash away the hurt and shame and embarrassment that embedded itself deep within the crevices of my human body. The hurt would dig its way into my pours like auto mechanic grease would underneath fingernails, I wanted to deeply and so freely to hate white people for what they overall orchestrated simply because they (whites) did not want their children to attend the same schools as theirs. I was dumb founded, vivid and to say the least .... ed off, still I learned to hide it.

Thank God I had a great and fantastic mom who always said, it's not right to hate regardless what they say or do. I knew that whenever I had the opportunity to leave Prince Edward County, Farmville, Virginia, I vowed never to return again to live. I would only return from time to time to visit my parents. Once God would call their number, I really would not have a reason to return to the area. Wow, in 1973 I graduated from high school and always hoped to attend college somewhere, but my parents were in need (mom always said, don't say that we are poor).

When I graduated from college (Alpha Phi Alpha Fraternity, Inc., awarded me an academic scholarship and low and behold, I convinced him to attend my commencement exercise. See dad never liked to drive a lot. I'm not sure if I would have forgiven him for not attending my graduation, but I had to keep it all bottled up, just like I had to vacate Farmville, VA (actually Prospect, VA is where we lived) because I still was in pain and shame about the schools closing, but that too I had to keep it all bottled up.

Here it is 2015 and somewhere between the 50's and now, I had to unbottle what has been bottled for such a long painful time for me. Yes, I'm ok now, really, I am. I have forgiven everyone who I felt was hurt by this ordeal, white people and even me, yes, I had to forgive me, unlock my mental doors and understand and accept why things were like they were back then, and every so often I think back to what my mom would say, (and dad would just listen). Don't hate white people, even the racist ones. God don't want you to hate." Yes, today I don't hate white people or any other race of people for what they may have done or want to do. I don't hate Prince Edward, Farmville, VA bottom line, I just don't want to ever come back to live in the area, no lie.

Darlene Jenkins Jordan

When school closed, I was not yet school age. When I heard that school had closed, I didn't know what to think. I wondered when I would get to go to school. I stayed home and my mother taught us as best she could. I still have the Bible my mother read stories to me and my siblings from. My mother did domestic work.

When school re-opened, I went to school for the first time in P. E. County. I started in the 2nd grade even though I had never attended school before.

Even though schools were closed, I was determined to become a nurse. During my years in Prince Edward schools, I was skipped several times and I graduated at age 17 in 1971 and went on to attend nursing school at Southside Community Hospital. Nursing school was not easy. There were only 5 Blacks in a class of 71.

Now, I am a retired Licensed Practical Nurse. I worked at Southside Community Hospital for 39.5 years before retiring. I got to do my dream job. I wanted to be a nurse since I was a child.

John Ross

When school closed, I was 2 years old, not old enough to go to school. I was living with my grandmother. I found out about the school closing through my siblings and my aunts, they got sent home and they didn't go back to school. We all were at home. I felt was I going to be able to go to school? Were they going to open the school again? We worked the fields, tobacco and corn fields and stuff and we helped around the house, we had nowhere to go, we had no education. My grandparents had very little education.

When school reopened, I was going on eight years old and I was put into the first grade and I missed two years of school. They wouldn't put us up in a grade, so I had to do first grade all over. I did the first grade and the second grade at Worsham Elementary School. After that my mama came home in the summer of '66. She said she was going to take me to New York, so I went to New York to live with my mother. When I got to New York, they wouldn't accept the grades I had down here, so I went to a Catholic School, St. Ambrose and I had to start the first and second grade all over again. I was nine years old; I was in the first and second grade. I left the Catholic School and went to a public school up there. I did the 4th, 5th and 6th grade in New York at PS45 public school. I left there and came back home to live with my grandmother and I have been here ever since.

I started the 7th grade at Prince Edward County High School. I stayed in school, and finished. In order for us, praise God, to get on track because we were getting older and in the wrong grade. The principal worked with us; I never did do the 11th grade in school. I skipped the 11th grade and went to the 12th, and it wasn't because of my education, it was because of my age. I would have been too old to be in school, but I still graduated when I was 19 years old. Now I work for the state. I am an assistant food service director. I love cooking and food. I went to a culinary school when I was at Longwood and they shipped me to Philadelphia for three weeks and I passed the culinary class, so cooking is my passion,

I own my own catering business. I am very proud of it, and very successful. I have opened up my own restaurant in the past years, due to the economy; I had to close that down. Things got tight in 2008 and 2009. Right now, I am doing ok. If school had not closed, the only problem I have in life, I am very good in math and I find now on my job the things I do in the world by computer and email. I have a hard time spelling, never learned the phonics or any kind of verbal language to talk or to spell. Most of my spelling now comes from memory. I would just like for people to know, and I am not a grudging person. I don't hold grudges. I just hope would never see it happen again. We learn from our pass to keep our future going. If I could keep this from happening again, I am all for it. That is what I would like to see happen.

David Wadsworth Topp

When school closed, I had not started school. I was supposed to start school that year in 1959 and that is when they closed the school. I found out about the school closing from my mother. At the time I didn't know any better, I was happy

78

because I didn't have to go to school. At the same time I was devastated, to be serious, because I did want to go because my mother had home schooled us to a point. She did it through the time when the school was closed 59-63, but things weren't the same anymore after schools did close. After school closed, my family and I stayed in Prince Edward County in Farmville, because we couldn't afford to go anywhere else. Daddy had tried to get us in schools out in Charlotte County, but the lady whose house we would have stayed at, we felt she was charging too much money. At that time $45.00 a week for three kids was a lot of money.

When school reopened, the first day, which was in 1963, of course I was excited. It was something I had never done before and when I went in it was all unfamiliar to me. So we just did what we were told to do, sit where we were told. We were in the auditorium and they would call our names to what class we were going to. In 1963 I was in the first grade. They never put me in the right grade, from 63-64, I went from the 1st grade to the 4th grade. I should have been in the 5th grade, but my homeroom teacher, Ms. Rainer felt like I should go to the 4th, so that is where I went.

Now I am disabled. I live in upper Marlboro, Maryland. I'm at home every day trying to survive. I was too young to think of what I would have done if school had not closed, but the fact that they didn't give me an opportunity to and when they sent me to school and let me go, they kind of rushed me through, I didn't really learn a lot while I was there and I just feel like I was cheated. I still feel like I was cheated because I was only in school from 63-73 and I graduated not knowing a lot of things. I could read and write, but math, science, biology and all of that stuff, I wasn't good at, because they didn't have good instructors to teach it.

I think the school closing affected a lot of kids because, like me, I started when I was 9 years old, but you had some people in my class that were as old as 15. It was like that all the way through school and they weren't really teaching us. They were pushing us through. I feel like they was getting us out of school for the public schools that they wanted. We were at an all-black high school and the year after I graduated I came back and I saw just as many if not more whites there than blacks. So I feel like we were pushed out of the way to get the school system ready for that generation of people to come through.

The apology that we got form Governor Warner, I think it was a good gesture, but the town of Farmville, the governors' office, if they ready wanted to show us how remorseful they were about what happened, they would open up their state universities and colleges to our kids and let our kids receive a free education, something that we were not afforded an opportunity to and this little token of money that they gave when Governor Warner made this gesture. That's all it was, a token and a gesture. I don't think it was done in good faith and I feel that if they really wanted to show us how remorseful, how sorry they were for treating us like that, like I said they should open up the community colleges and universities to our kids and let our kids receive that education that we didn't get. From what I understand they were only offering a certain amount of money to each individual and then you had to be in the state of Virginia in order to receive it. *(I informed him that money was not given, they allowed us to attend school tuition free).*

Jimmy Watson

When school closed, I was not old enough for school. I found out about the school closing from my parents and folks in the neighborhood. I was not old enough to really know what to think. I think I was too young to understand. When I was old enough my mother drove us to a church to go to school. I remember going to a church and learning my ABCs but I think it was in Prospect. When school re-opened, I returned to school. I was in the first grade.

My father did construction work and my mother did babysit and sometimes she worked in a nursing home.

Now I do mainly construction work. I always wanted to do a lot of different things and I never settled on just one thing. I was mostly interested in electronics and I wanted to know why and how things worked. I remember not wanting to go to the school at the church. Once I started to go, I found that I could learn. The more I learned; the more I wanted to know.

A few children left before school closed as a result of the firing of their parent, who was involved in the PTA and the fight for equal schools. This left a sadness for their classmates in realizing they would not be with them.

Shirley Elaine Lancaster - Gholston

When the schools closed, we had already moved from Farmville in 1957, which was after my father lost his job due to his involvement in the desegregation efforts to get a new school. He was fired, I believe in 1955, he sold insurance and we remained here in Farmville for a year and a half and then the beginning of 1957, as a family we moved to Maryland, Southern Maryland, Saint Mary's County Maryland and that's where I grew up after that period of time. When I left Farmville, I was in the 3rd. grade, when school actually closed, I was finishing 5th grade in Maryland or going into 6th grade. I remember my dad talking about it. I remember maybe reading the Farmville Herald. I am not certain, because he did continue to get the paper and we continued to come to Farmville summers and in between times for visits with friends. So in hearing about the schools closing it was kind of surreal. I was an 11 year old. And then as 11 years old would do, I went ahead with my merry little life and didn't think a lot about it.

The friends that I still had contact with were not in Farmville any longer. I did know, for example, the Madison's, who were very good friends of ours and I knew that they had moved to Chester Town Maryland. I knew that Naja Griffin and Cocheyse and others had to go to school somewhere else. I think they were there for a while. It was unclear in my mind what everybody was going to be doing and where they were going to be. There was just this sadness and sort of disbelief that this could have happened, and that it did happen.

When school reopened, I was in Junior high or at the beginning of high school. I remember different stages along the line and different years when I would hear from my dad the steps that were being taken to open the schools. I remember hearing, and it seemed to me that it was at least two times, possible even in the summer when we thought, oh, the schools are going to open in September because there had been a ruling that indicated that the schools would have to be open. Then September would come around and due to some kind legal changes and the appeals and other kinds of events that occurred, the schools didn't open. I heard about the Free Schools. I remember thinking when the Free Schools opened, that was the year schools were supposed to be opened. Then I read and my dad talked about the fact that the Free Schools were not the public schools. But then again, it didn't really hit me, and none of the real brunt of the school closing hit me personally as it would have, as it did as I am sure most of my friends in Farmville, because I wasn't there. I didn't experience it first hand, I only heard about it indirectly.

I graduated in Maryland, I went on to College, University of Maryland and then began working in the school system of Prince George County of Maryland. I worked as an educator, a Special Education Teacher and Supervisor and Resource Teacher, that sort of thing in Prince George County, Maryland from 1970 – 2000. I retired in 2000 and I began working for an educational company that distributes books to schools and many school systems and the like and that is what I am still doing. I'm ready to retire from that at this time. (laughing)

Well, the biggest lost that I feel is the loss of connection with the friends that I really lost before the schools closed, because had my dad not been fired from his job because of his actions and involvement with the PTA and with the entire education push to have public schools that were equal for all children, had that not occurred we would have grown up in Farmville. I would have lived in that little house across the street from this museum, probably until we lived somewhere else or would have still lived there and I would have grown up with Naja and Dorothy Madison and all the other young people that were, that were my friends. We moved because this was coming, we just left before it came and that was the biggest difference, I think.

John G. Lancaster, Jr.

 Well we left two years before the schools closed, so I didn't learn about the schools closing until it actually happened and I remember seeing it, first on the news. That was when I first learned that they had really closed. My reaction, probably disbelief because I like so many others, especially those that were here and didn't think that was possible for them to really do it. Then once it happened, I think everyone had the hope that they would open, you know, like soon. Then of course as the decision was pushed through the courts, and the decision came down, I think that everyone thought that schools would open immediately. Of course that was not the case.

When we left Farmville in 1957, we moved to Lexington Park, Maryland, which is 50 miles south of Washington, D.C. When the schools reopened, we did not return to Farmville. We continued to live in Maryland. In 1959, I would have been in the 6th or 7th grade.

I am retired from the airline industry. I started working with North West Airlines in 1969 and retired from the airline industry in 2005. I also worked as a children's counselor in Brooklyn, New York for about three years, but I work part time now as a Real Estate Assistant or an Independent Real Estate Assistant in Sans Francisco, California That's what I do now, very part time.

The school closing didn't really affect me, but I share my sister's sentiment when I look at pictures of the Baker boys, and Albert Rawlings and the Madison's and Herbert Brown and all my friends, Skip Griffin, all of my acquaintances, you know that would have continued, but that was that was not to be.

The only thing I would like to add is that I would like to see that the story be continually told. This is something that can't be forgotten. It needs to be told over and over and over and over again, because when I see the reaction from people who see the video for the first time or see the MSNBC's Special, they somehow get to Moton, and they learn the story. It's like (pause) this couldn't have happened. What do you mean this happened, because it's not in history books and if it hadn't been for Brown v Board of Education's 50th Anniversary, I think that was when it really became public. If you live in Virginia or if you live in Farmville, that's one thing, but from another state, this is all new and sometimes I guess, almost unbelievable. If you would tell someone that this happened, they would just say, no way, no way, they could not have closed schools for that long. They did, so continue to tell the story. My hat is all to who keeps this alive, to think that it started on the back of a 16-year-old fearless little girl, is just amazing to me, but I appreciate being a part of it.

Now, put yourself in the place of this scenario. Waiting your entire life for the day to attend school for the first time just to find out that your school is closed. Being six years old when school closed and when it reopened, you are 11 years old going to school for the first time in the first grade.

Barbara Hicks- Spring

I wasn't in a grade when school closed. I hadn't started school. I would have been able to start that year, but because you had to be six years old to start school and the way my birthday fell, I couldn't go to school the year I should have. So I had to wait, I was seven by the time school closed so therefore, by the time

I reached seven years of age, the schools closed up. I don't know how I found out about the school closing. Because at such an early age, I never really never thought about it, maybe just from hearing it through my brothers and sisters. I really didn't have a reaction, I guess because of my age and being so young, you never thought about the importance of having an education and going to school. When school closed, first of all we didn't go anywhere, we just worked in the tobacco fields. My daddy was like a sharecropper I guess and he was raising tobacco for someone else. So, we would help them and then in summer time we would work for this white guy who had tobacco.

My fourth year, the year before the free school started, I went away to Ashton, Virginia for a short period of time, but I didn't stay. The gentlemen that I was staying with began to abuse me, so I told my mother and my mother brought me back home.

So, I don't know how long I was there. The only thing I remember, we went a little while in the basement at the First Baptist Church for a little bit. I remember we would walk five miles over to High Rock Baptist to a little school there and we went to school there for a short period of time. I don't remember how long until Free school reopen and I went to Mary E. Branch #2 in Farmville, Virginia. I was 11 years old when I first started school. As far as I can remember, they ended up putting me in the 5th grade, why I don't know.

Now I am a retired firefighter. I used to be a police officer for a short period of time. In addition to that after retiring from the Fire Department, my husband and I traveled throughout the United States doing missionary work.

I never really thought about what I wanted to be if school had not closed, I was too young to think about it then. I never even thought about what I wanted to be. I guess it was because of things that took place. I never thought about it. I guess the only thing I can say is that maybe school closing was a blessing and it could have been a curse. A blessing if school had never been closed, I might have not had the opportunities that I took advantage of, but if the schools had remained open, then I might have stayed here in Prince Edward and end up in a mediocre job like a lot of other people did.

Catherine Johnson Jackson

When school closed, I was looking forward to going to school, it would have been my first year of school. When school was opened, I thought I would be going to school. I was very excited, very excited, I am going to school, that's what I thought. And when my mom told me, no, they closed school, you are not going to school, it was sort of like this real sadness came over me. I remember when my older brother and sisters, were in school, a one room school house and I went to school with them one day, and I just felt so good to be there. I was happy and I can't wait to go to school, I was thinking, you know (laughing), but it didn't happen.

After school closed, well it was the students that had come to town to teach the ones who didn't get a chance to go out of town for an education. Go to another county, I should say for an education. There was a very sweet girl, I never will forget her, at the time I didn't wear glasses and I could barely see anything, and she took me to get my first pair of glasses, yea and after I got them on and I could really see. It was just like a whole new world. I don't remember her name, but I will always remember the person who did it for me. So, we were taught like in the church basement at First

Baptist Church and we also had some classes at the AME Church across the street.

Well, when school reopened, of course I was glad again. I was happy again. I was going to school. We were already learning, they were teaching us at the church and what not, but I would be in a regular class with kids, just getting to know people and you know, a regular teacher, a regular class. I missed time out of school, but when we did go to school, I guess for a whole year, they evaluated us and placed us in a grade. I wasn't in a grade when school closed, they placed me in like in the third grade, so I was nine in the third grade, you know.

Now I am retired from Prince Edward County Schools. I was there for a total of nine years. If school had not closed, well you know what I would have liked to have done was to have been a teacher.

In some cases, after school closed occasionally, a few children were taught by their parents or family members who were teachers or others. They were able to continue their education, although informal. At this period of time Home Schooling was not an accredited way of receiving your education. It just goes to show how much our education was valued and what lengths parents would go to prevent it being denied to their children. Here are a few of their stories.

Gary W. Smith

My mother was a teacher so she taught me pre-k. School closed before I was in the first grade. I was not old enough to go to school when school closed. I found out that school was closed because I had older siblings who were in school and a brother that went away to school when school closed. The rest of us stayed home. My father owned property in Cumberland, so we switched to Green Creek Elementary school in Cumberland County which was a one room schoolhouse. I believe I did the first and second grade. When school reopened, I started Free School. I believe I was at about the 3rd or 4th grade. I started at Mary E. Branch #1, and then I went to Mary E. Branch #2 and then to R. R. Moton High School. It was changed to Prince Edward County High School in my senior year; I graduated from Prince Edward County High School.

Well, the closing of the school was pretty much a slap in the face in my view as this was a conservative town and Jim Crow laws were in effect back then, segregation and all of that. It was just an additional comment on the state of affairs in Virginia at that time, that Black people were not good enough and that Black people were considered second class citizens at that time presented a challenge. I had to adjust to my adult life.

Now I am in a business with my wife. We own Catherine's Waterside Adult Care.

Margaret Allen Stiff

When school closed, I was in the 6th grade. I found out about the closing of the schools on the news that school was closed and we were not going to school in September. When I heard that school was closed, being a kid, I said we will go back soon. When school closed round in the surrounding community, which is Hampden Sydney community we had classes in the basement of Mercy Seat Church. My grandmother who is Mrs. Margaret Allen Harris was one of the teachers. There was quite a few other teachers around there at the time. After about two years my dad and mom got up with a lady about something that Reverend Griffin had, and I was the oldest girl and my oldest brother, which was my brother Johnny. We went up to Warren, Virginia, where we went to school and stayed with Ms. Leola Downy. When school reopened, I came back to Prince Edward County and went to the Free School. I was in the 9th grade. I graduated from Moton High School in 1968 because they hadn't changed over to Prince Edward County High School.

I am retired as of now. Since I retired, I went to school for a while and took computer and came out with a 93, which I thought was good. I did a little home care for a woman, but every day it is something to do for parts of the family or some place to go. When I graduated from school, I was planning on going to nursing school in Jersey. My cousins James, said come and live with me. You know, you grown, in love; it was just one of those things. When I first came out of high school, I worked at this place called Stack Pole Company and after that I went to work at a place called Thomasville in Appomattox, Virginia. I worked in sales and the shoe department, in which I enjoyed and the years just went on by. I think I came out pretty good, although I missed a couple years out of school. I found a job, got married and been married for 40 some years now. My husband William also was a person that was affected by the school closing. When school closed, he went to Appomattox, Virginia. After that he went to Virginia State University and Norfolk State University where he got his learning. He went 2 years there.

Janet Elizabeth Crawley - Gardener

 I was 13 years old and in the seventh grade when school closed. I don't remember how I found out about the school closing. When I heard about it, I was upset because schools were closed and hey, how am I going to complete my education, what will we do now? You know, I was upset, totally upset about it. I was really disappointed and hurt.

After the school closed, we didn't do anything right away. When I did go to school Mrs. Victoria Brown was teaching in Appomattox. She came past our house and picked up me and my brother James. I don't know if my sister and my brother Ralph went or not, but I know that my brother James and I rode to Appomattox with her to go to school there at Carver Price.

When school reopened, we came back, because she only taught up there because schools were closed here. She taught here in Prince Edward County, so in order for us to go to school, well she had a job and she knew that we were out of school, so in order for us to have some type of education she was going and transported us. It's four of us. I am the oldest, my brother James and then Ralph and Ann all came back to school. I started back in high school at R. R. Moton. I didn't graduate but I had completed the 11th grade and gone into the 12th grade, because I got a picture of me in my cap and gown.

Right now, I am working for Home Recovery as a Personal Care Aide. If school had not closed, I had dreams. I would have returned to school and graduated, got my diploma and I had thought about going to nursing school, beautician school. I had thought about a lot of things I wanted to do. I would like to add, by the school closing and my life going on, and I did get my GED, I did go to work, I did more or less things that I wanted to do, but one thing I have learned from school being closing is that it was just a period of time in my life and it was a door that was closed at that time. I have learned that just because I didn't get what I wanted then, the door is still open now for me to go to college. You know what I mean; the door was opened for me to go back and get my diploma, if I hadn't gotten my GED and now if I want to go to college I can. I can do anything now that I want because I had that foundation in the elementary school and in the high school and now you can get tutored, you know what I'm saying? Doors are open for me or anybody. Just because we lost sometime, doesn't we are completely lost. We can go forward into the future. It's not like you know I was just bogged down and I couldn't rise. I was down and I couldn't get up. I am up, I am up, I'm up and I have gone to Charlotte County to the Adult class.

In 1960, organizations such as the Quakers and the American Friends Service Committee began efforts to send Black students who were denied education in Prince Edward County out of the county for their education. PECCA, Reverend L. Francis Griffin, Reverend A.I. Dunlap, a minister of African Methodist Episcopalian Church, who taught at Kittrell, and was instrumental in providing for the children to be transported and attend Kittrell College. One of the main goals was to get the juniors and seniors into places or homes in order to allow them to graduate. As different organizations and groups began to find homes for children, the town of Farmville was left resembling that of a ghost town. Sadly, for various reasons a number of children did not get a chance to leave home or left before obtaining their diploma.

Clyde Hamlin

I passed to the 12th grade when school closed. I would say I found out at home, probably my parents. What was your reaction when I heard that school was closed.

Well I was disappointed, because I was going into my senior year. After school closed, well I stayed here in Virginia, but I worked with my father for a year before I went into the military. When school reopened, oh I was on active duty in the military career.

Now I am sitting at home retired (laughing). Well, I retired from the Air Force in 1981, then I retired totally from civil service in 2000. If school had not closed, I probably would have been a logger, well put it this way a logger or into the service, one of the other. Probably into the service first, then a logger.

What you would like to add? Well nothing really, I was disappointed, a lot of people got put out behind it, but personally for me it was good for me because I got out of Dodge and I am glad I did.

Christine Irving Watkins

I was in the 11th grade when school closed. I had just passed to the 12th grade. I lived a year here and a year with my dad. At this time, I was with my dad in New York, but I got angry with my dad and I came home to go to the 12th grade and school was closed. So *they* told me to go the Methodist Church to Reverend Dunlap, and Reverend Dunlap took me to Kittrell College in North Carolina. I was supposed to bring him some money, but I didn't have any money. I didn't have a dime and when I went up there, he said, didn't I tell you to bring some money, and I said I don't have it and he was nice enough to give me some money. Reverend Dunlap always made sure that those of us that were poor and I was poor at that time. He would come by and bring peas, can corn or whatever things we needed.

I stayed at Kittrell and graduated. I found out about the schools closing when I came down and tried to get in. I felt terrible. I felt that why would they close the schools because of somebody's color? That is truly what I thought, because I had been in New York all that time and I came back and I couldn't believe it. You know, some people could go to school and some people couldn't.

I am a retired nurse and after my husband died, I moved back to Virginia about 4 years ago. I still travel back to New York where my children and grandchildren and great grandchildren live. I love down here. I would love for school to have stayed open because my brother was not able to go to school, was not able to go to Kittrell because somebody had to stay home and work. That's how things were back in the day. My brother Bobby is a year younger than me, but he has educated himself, he has moved up and he's got a nice place and doing quite well, thank God. It is something that should have never happened to children, because it left a scar that will last for a long time. I know that Virginia is trying, but some things need a little time to heal, you know.

Robert Hamlin
I don't remember being fore warned as the school year in the spring of 1959 ended, that schools may not continue in the fall of 1959. Like normal we all said our goodbyes for

the summer expecting to meet again in the fall. I was looking forward to my 12th grade year. As the summer moved on the rumors began to circulate that black children might not have school in the Fall, while the white children would have school. My feelings were that they could not and would not do that. When Labor Day passed and we were not back in school I was hurt. Like most kids I didn't mind an extra week or so of extended summer vacation. After that I began to worry that I might not get to finish school. Mrs. Rawlins had recommended that I be accepted into the National Honor Society and I was looking forward to that. When schools did not open, I don't know what happed to those records and I never heard from that organization.

During that time, my Dad was away from home during the week. His business was cutting pulpwood in Northern Virginia. So, he was only home during the weekends and my mom didn't drive. Since we lived out in Rice, we didn't get information in a timely manner about anything that might have been going on. Also, we did not have a telephone. Everything was by word of mouth.

Near the end of September, I spent a week in Northern Virginia with my dad. When I came home at week's end my mom told me that Flossie Oliver (Flossie Moore) wanted to see me on Saturday. So, we went and visited with them. Our families were close friends. That's when I found out about Kittrell Junior College. She had already enrolled and was attending for about 2 weeks.

My Parents took me to Kittrell the next day and got me enrolled. I was so relieved. I had been in pain thinking that I had struggled all those years and not get to graduate High School. My Parents had so wanted that for me because Dad had only gone to the 7th grade while finished 6th grade. Those were the highest grades offered at their respective schools. I did graduate High School at Kittrell and I stayed and graduated Junior College there as well. School Closing was a temporary setback but it did not stop me. Instead it motivated me.

I hold 3 Associate Degrees (Kittrell, Community College of the Airforce and Indiana University) and a Bachelor's of General Studies with emphasis in Social and Behavioral Sciences. I enjoyed a very successful career for 20 years in the United States Airforce and another 20 years in managing employment and training programs in both Indiana and Virginia working with people who needed to get skills for better paying jobs. I've had a happy life. The end!

Grace C. Logan

When school closed, I would have been in the 12th grade. I would have finished school when it reopened. I found out

about the school closing by hearing my mom and other people talking about it. When I heard that school had closed, I was very upset, I couldn't understand why they would close the school, because no one had talked to us and we didn't know anything that was going on. We had no information of anything except that there would be no more school. When school closed, I went to work in Prince Edward in Farmville. Whatever came along to the free schools, like the churches, one brother was sent away.

When school reopened, I did not go back, I continued working. I am retired and a minister of the gospel. If school had not closed, I always wanted to do nursing, that was my goal. Nursing and teaching were my desires for my life. I didn't get it that way, but I am now able to teach the word of God, so I am still teaching. The school closing was hard for my family, because my mother was the only, as we would say, the bread winner and my brother and I went to work, so we could help her out and she did not want to talk about it because she was afraid of losing her job. So everything was a hush, hush in our household. Nobody talked about it, my mother just went along with whatever they told her to do. And if there was some place for her children to go to get an education, like the teaching in the churches or whoever opened up a place for them, this is what my brothers and sisters did. It really affected my sisters and brothers. I am able to cope with it, but they have problems accepting the racial discrimination and what we feel has done to us. I think that we should not just let it go, but learn from it so the same mistake is not made again. I think our younger people should learn what took place with us and they should try to do better. I really have a hard time with the young people now because I see the opportunities that they have that we did not have. They often do not take advantage them. So I wonder what more can do to help them.

Grace Simms –Foulks

I was in the 11th grade when school closed. I found out about the school closing from a neighbor and another lady where I lived. I felt awful when I heard that school was closed, because it was my last year. I wanted to graduate and that is why I went to Kittrell, North, Carolina so I could graduate my 12th grade year. After I graduated at Kittrell, I went to New York and I've been there ever since. I am retired now; I used to work in the post office in New York. Now, I have moved back down here. I don't know what to say about the school closing. It felt awful, you know because I knew that was my last year and I really wanted to graduate. I feel bad about it.

Charles I. Taylor, Sr.

 When school closed, I was in the 11th grade and I had just graduated to the 12th. I found out about the school closing when I was working in Atlantic City, New Jersey, I came back home and all the kids were gone, because I didn't get back home until sometime the 7th or 8th of September, and my mother told me then, because we didn't have telephones, and cell phones. We didn't do any texting and that type of stuff, that there was not going to be any school. I had not heard that entire summer that it wouldn't be any schools. When I heard that school was closed, my reaction was that I couldn't believe it, there is no such thing. This can't be true. I couldn't understand you not being able to go to school. It was a total shock.

When school closed, I got to go to Kittrell Junior College in North Carolina, under the AME. AME is the African Methodist Episcopalian Church, had a minister here A.I. Dunlap who taught at Kittrell. He convinced Frank Madison Reid, Sr., to open up a high school program or to enlarge it, they had a small one, I think, about 10 or 20 kids, and he told him our condition and that he wanted to bring some kids from Farmville down to go to the high school, and that the AME would basically fund part of our tuition. I think they talked to Rev. Dunlap, he told them he just wanted to bring the seniors, but the bishop agreed, so quickly, he said can I bring some juniors too? He said, I guess I can, and he said what about some sophomores, so from 12 people, it turned out to be 60 of us. I went down to

Rev. Griffin on a Friday afternoon, we left Farmville and they took me alone, and when I got there, I think most of the kids were happy to see me because I was the class clown. I was the basketball and baseball captain and they were so happy to see that now it was another piece of the puzzle. Each time somebody came, because throughout the year, people who found out about how to get there, came in, so pieces of the puzzle, Sam Jackson and Levy Lambert, and those guys who tried to go to other schools, but when they found out that they were from Prince Edward County, they kicked them out, so they ended up coming to Kittrell, so we got together there.

When school reopened, I had graduated, got married, had children; it didn't take me long to do what I needed to do. I was in the military, Vietnam in 1963. I was in the army for 24 years as the Senior Specialist Psychologist for the Walter Reid Army Institute of Research. I did research on human behavior; race relations and you name it. So, I did that and then I went to Germany to do substance abuse for H. Norman School Swachcloth and I went over to be the senior counselor of drug and alcohol rehabilitation center for patients. I got out of the army, my 20 years was up, and came back to New Port News; I had to give them a year, and you can't just leave from one place to another and come out and say I quit, because you are based on slots, so I stayed there for one year and then I went to work at the oldest and largest State Mental Institution State Mental Institute in the United States, Eastern State Hospital in Williamsburg, Virginia and I headed their long term mental rehabilitation program; I did that for twenty some years and did a lot of things there. I have been retired from the State Institution for 9 years, doing volunteering in mental health and hospice program; I work with people that are dying.

If school had not closed, I wanted to be the basketball

coach at R.R. Moton for 25 years. That's what I wanted to be; I wanted to be another Mr. Truman, that's all I wanted to do was to coach sports and to go out and get the kids and teach them right down here on this field. (We were sitting in the building Charles attended when school closed, now the Moton Museum) I wanted to relive my old coach's life, because I thought it was a wonderful life, how he had come here and got us and put us together with summer stuff and gave us a purpose. I think sports transcend racism, and property and everything else, because that field out there was our playground. That's all we had, and he made that an important part of our lives.

Every time I come here, I look down there and I have flashbacks, of the days we use to drag that field, because the city didn't help us with anything. So we did everything; picking up the rocks and gravels and making it somewhat safe and all the other stuff. I wanted to come back and become head coach of baseball and basketball of R.R. Moton for 25 years and then just ride off into the sunset. I had said many times to many people, thousands and thousands of people about our school closing, and I never had the bitterness that a lot of people had.

I learned more of how to deal with life from the school closing. I used to tell a lot of people, if you can go through what we went through, all this other stuff is a piece of cake. I have anger and frustration with white people and I learned so much about why things were that way they were. See if you had asked me at 17, I wouldn't have known how the system worked. They didn't teach us the system. We weren't smart enough to know the system. I think I was smart enough to listen to Rev. Griffin, because I lived next door and went to church every Sunday with him and heard him talk about it, the school boards and all that stuff like that, so therefore I came into a state of exceptions about our conditions. See we learned, me and your husband learned long ago, that discrimination was going to be there, but we can still have fun. We can enjoy the hand that was dealt to us, that's another way I use to tell people, that hand was dealt to me and I picked it up and looked at it and I say who, I wanted to turn it back in because it had no winners. We had to make winners out of a hand that looked like, that no one wanted, no one wanted to be discriminated, no one wanted to walk from the end of main street, all the way up here to get on the same bus that passed you and then go all the way up there and then come back and no television and radio, no communication, no say.

We had no voice or we didn't think we had a voice, because there was Barbara Johns, who did her thing and in 1951, that showed that you can have a voice, but we didn't follow through with that voice and I didn't follow through, basically because once I left, I ran into a life I never expected, to be able to work for Generals and be on staff and make decisions and to be the only black person in there. It was almost like, unless I had a say, they didn't close the meeting. I had to have a say, my input, and then when I got out of the military, I had to go and change some segments of the State Institution on what

I learned in the army. I was working in psychiatry when I was in the army and once you find something you love doing and when I got out of the army, I found the largest State Mental Institution in Virginia, it was just like falling into a bed of roses. There was no limit and I had learned that our education was second class in many ways, the books, the opportunities and the lack of facilities, things that we didn't have here. Somehow, I was able to overcome that and sometimes I question myself. How was I able to do that because I have a condition that causes me to read things three or four times to get an understanding. I am dyslexics and no one ever knew that I was, but that made me study hard, read it two or three times to process it. I read, reverse stuffs, numbers and all stuff.

During and before 1962 children were still without a school and the U.S. Department of Justice files a friend of the court brief on behalf of the NAACP in their appeal of the closing of the Prince Edward County schools. Parents were desperately struggling to figure out what to do. There were some who found places to send their children, many who did not and others who rented houses in other counties. Here are those children's stories.

Edward Thornton

I had passed to the 3rd grade when school closed. I am not sure how I found out, I was only eight years old, probably from my parents and cousins. I was kind of shocked, bewildered and not understanding what was really happening, with unanswered questions about no school to attend.

I missed the first two years. In the third year I went to Stafford County, Virginia for one month, but returned to Farmville after that month. My mother was doing house work cooking for a family in Farmville where the husband was a member of the Cumberland County School Board. He allowed me to enroll in the Cumberland County System. The school name was "Green Creek Elementary School, "a one room school where the grades 1st–5th were being taught. After crossing the Appomattox River to catch the school bus to school, once arriving, the teacher asked me what grade was I in? I said the fourth and that's where I started, I had talked while on the bus of some friends and they said they were in the fourth, so I said the same.

When school reopened, I returned to the Prince Edward County School System. I had passed to the 6th grade.

I have been working as an accountant for over forty years. Numbers have always been my passion, math was my favorite subject, I am very satisfied with my occupation. The school closing made me have a fulfilled life in spite of obstacles place in front of you.

John Lacy Jenkins

I was in the 4th grade when school closed. I found out about the school closing, the following year, I was supposed to go to Mary E. Branch. I was a big kid, I got to ride the bus, but the bus never came. How did I feel when I found out school was closed? At that age you don't really know how to feel, but now that I am older; it was a tragedy, it was an injustice. I have some very strong feelings about what type of government would allow a group of people to discriminate against in such a manner. When school closed I went to jobs and we had this thing called the free school in learning centers that we would go to, it wasn't accredited by the state, it was something in the Hampton District that the community put together so we wouldn't be lacking so far in our education.

When school opened, I returned to school; I was two or three grades behind. I was twenty-one when I graduated from R.R. Moton High School. I tell people that now and they look at me like you must have been a slow kid. A lot of people that I work with when we get to talking about our education and I tell them that I was a product of the school closing and they seem to be amazed. They can't fathom it you know.

I am a retired state worker. Right now, I work for the Daily Planet. I am the manager of a homeless shelter. If school had not closed, I really don't know, that is a very difficult question to answer. I could say I would like to have been a lawyer, doctor or something along those lines, but I would have been professional person regardless.

Rosa Redd- Street

I was in the third grade when school closed. I found out about the school closing when my grandparents told me. Being young, I really wasn't concerned about school closing, I just thought they would always be open. It didn't make sense to me, I just thought that that particular school was closing and we were going to another school. I was going to Mount Lee School in Meherrin, Virginia where I lived. My teacher's name was Mrs. White and I was happy in school.

When school closed my grandparents decided that we would go to Baltimore to go to school, so the small ones were sent to Baltimore, Maryland to go to school and the older ones were sent to Kittrel, North Carolina to go to school. When school reopened, I was happy for one thing because I had cousins who didn't get a chance to go to school, I was coming out of high school graduating from the 12th grade and thinking about what I was going to do next, go to college or work. After school closed, I worked for the federal government for 40 years. I retired in 2010 and now I am just enjoying retirement.

If school hadn't closed, I would like to have stayed in Virginia. I was born here, the people that I loved was here.

Being sent away was traumatic for me at the time, but it was what had to be done at the time and my parents ..., but if I had stayed here, I would like to work for the people here and do something to help the people in Virginia. I hope we do not face another prejudice situation like that, it didn't make any sense than, it doesn't make any sense now. It's hard to compensate people and give that time back and it just uprooted so many families until it was just a big question mark as to why, and of course there are no answers to anything like that.

Thomas Jackson

 I was in the 4th grade when school closed. I found out about the school closing when somebody told us that school was closed. I didn't understand it. I was young then. I can't really remember who told me, but the word got around. When I heard about it, back then kids were young and it was kind of a glad thing in the beginning because kids didn't want to go to school anyway, but we didn't know it was going to hurt us in the long run.

When school closed, I didn't really go anywhere, we just stayed home and worked on the farm. Then I went to Peaks School in Prospect right down the road from my house. When the Free School reopened, I didn't go back to the same school, I went back to Mary E. Branch II in Farmville. I got skipped to the 6th grade. I am retired now from the Prince Edward County School System; drove the school bus for 34 years. I graduated from Prince Edward County High School. When I first started it was R. R, Moton and later on, it changed to Prince Edward County Public Schools.

Melvin M. Baker

I was in the third grade when school closed. I found out about the school closing from my parents. My reaction when school closed, glad, I thought I didn't have to go to school anymore.

When school closed, I moved to Centreville, Md., where my father found a position as a teacher. I continued my education there. When school reopened, I returned to school in Farmville in 1967. I was in the 11th grade. I graduated from R. R. Moton High School on June 8, 1968.

I am retired from D.C. Department of Corrections from September 1977 to December 1999. I am not sure if there was any impact from the closure. I wish that this chapter of history had not needed to happen.

In 1964, the United States Supreme Court ruled that Prince Edward Public schools must reopen. A lot of children were still home due to the parents unable to find a place for them to go, did not feel comfortable with anyone with their children or just could not bear to have them away from them. Here you will not only read how this occurred, but what was occurring in the church, the town of Farmville, what the parents went through, and the effect it had on relationships.

Deloris Blanton- Hendricks

This interviewee gave not only what happened to her, but a full account of how the town was during that time.

I was in the 10th grade when school closed. I heard about the school closing in the newspaper and radio, my parents and word of mouth and from neighbor's friends. The whole town was lit up with it. I will never forget it. Lord, I will never forget it. I found out about it in our church. I knew it before it hit the papers. Reverend Griffin, he told us, he always kept us abreast of that political stuff, he told us everything, he told us every time they had an election, national and state. When I say national, he knew all about the Kennedy boys, where they got, what they got and he told us numerous times about don't do this and don't do the other, cause this one did this, and that one did the other.

Yea, that was his main thing to discuss, but he preached the gospel on that and he made sure we were informed about who to vote for. We could count on that. Reverend Ashton didn't do it. Reverend Ashton didn't discuss it like Reverend Griffin, he says the Lord is in control, but Reverend Griffin, not him.

When I heard that school was closed, I didn't believe it because I didn't want to believe it and others was saying how could that be that ain't so. How could that be, you know, they can't do that so I kept hopeful for a long time. I kept denying it, I did it until the last, I just denied it. Because it just didn't make sense that they could do a certain race of people that way and nobody could explain it and you know it's wrong but I kept hopeful. I didn't give in to it and say oh well no, in my mind, I said no, it ain't going to happen. I finally realized that it was going to happen, and it did. It was the last of whatever you call that, I knew, I got to give in now. I felt very hurt and confused, very confused because I never heard anything like this in my life and you just couldn't' make sense of it, I was wondering where did they get that power to do that, you know?

When school closed, I had to finally go to Cumberland

County because my mother wanted me to be with her relatives. Kittrell College she said was too far away and it was not enough supervision for people my age, so I had to give in and go there. I didn't want to go, even though it was my parents because they lived differently. I mean we were no elite people, but my grandparents lived, you know, they were just average people and at that time not many people in the rural area had electric lights and when I found out I had to study by lamp light. I told my mom I couldn't half way get my lesson at night, but that wasn't all of it. I just didn't want to be there in the bushes. My grandpa built his own house and this particular one wasn't that far back off the road, but the first one, Lord, it took you a day and a half to get to it. I just didn't like it. I didn't want to be that far off the road with people that old and nobody but me with them. If a bear had come it would have killed us all. I don't understand that until today why they were not afraid. I was sure at some point and time during those years, those bears came around that house, but by the grace of God, they did not bother us. I never did see one, but there were other kind of critters. I know that, yes, because it was too far.

I don't mean to speak harshly concerning my grandparents because I know they did the best they could just like all other people with their age and ability. I also realized that in speaking of the bears and being so afraid. I know we were kept safe form them by the grace of God. It was the same grace and mercy that did not allow the Klu Klux Klan at our doors to break them down and kill us. But they were there, oh how they were there. They were there, that's why the schools were closed. But God kept us safe and I am grateful, from the back woods to Longwood University, that's quite an adventure. Why my grandfather had built that house so far from the road, I'll never know. Maybe because they wouldn't sell him any more land. My mom and the rest had to laugh at that themselves.

When school reopened, I had finished school two years ago in Cumberland in 1961. I was working then. I didn't lose any time. Now I am retired and working with Head Start. After the system told me that I couldn't go, I said yes, I am, I graduated from Longwood. They didn't want us to finish high school or any school and then I was determined that I was going to finish, I was going to go, because I knew that living and working here in Farmville, that all Black folks could ever hope to do at Longwood was work in kitchen or dining area or cleaning and I was determined that I wasn't going to do either one. I made it, I did, and I can't say anything bad about anybody there at the time I attended, everybody was just as nice to me as they could be. No complaints, no complaints.

I still was hurt that I had to make any change, and I didn't have to go far as some students, but I was not with the family. It wasn't anything that I had done or anyone in my family, but something had happened to us that we did not want and I had to adjust and it wasn't easy because I had never lived away from home any long length of time. I had always visited my relatives and grandparents there, and if I wanted to spend the night that was my pleasure, but to be forced to do this is a different story.

I had some great expectations after attending the new school. It was built after the strike, oh, I thought I was in heaven. I went there in the 8th grade to the new high school and I went from the 8th to the 10th and I had no thought that I wouldn't be able to walk down that isle and walk across that stage and graduate. So, when I found out that I couldn't, you know that was a terrible blow. I had so many plans in my 10th grade year, but when I had to leave, I just lost all energy. There were so many things I wanted do, I wanted to always play an instrument. And I had decided what I wanted to play. Of course, I had always been in the choir, I loved music and I wanted to pursue whatever else they had to offer. I was hoping for other things to come because it was a new school.

Even though I know I was blessed, there were so many others who made my heart cry when I think about it today, it still hurts because they never went anywhere. Even today, I know that and I can imagine how they felt not having somewhere to go and I would ask some of them are you going to school this year, and they said no, and I wasn't old enough to comprehend and I still don't understand or else their parents didn't let them go, because they had to go so far away from them. But I hurt not just for me because I was still with loving people. There were changes in the household because of my absence and my dad had it almost worse than I because every Monday morning, I would get to the door. I would have to pack my bag overnight and with everything that I needed for the week, but he got so full, and that made me hurt because I saw him getting ready to tear up and I would cry because I didn't want to go.

My mom was strong and she would tell my daddy because he would come to the door and tell her don't make her go. She would tell him, you go sit down, this child is going out of here, she's got to get her education, what you think she going to do? Sit here the whole week and do nothing? But the look on his face, I knew he was hurting and that made me cry because he didn't want me to go, so it affected the family even though I wasn't going but maybe 25 miles down the road, it still broke the family union and that is why some other parents didn't' let their children go because they didn't want to separate from them. Overtime we heard stories where some children weren't treated well. But I thank the Lord, I thank my mom and my dad for my opportunity, but she was on the money, as soon as she knew, every fall everybody would be sitting at the radios, with their ears peeled to hear what the news was going to be, every year it was the same way, THE SCHOOLS IN PRINCE EDWARD COUNTY WILL BE CLOSED THIS YEAR, and every year my heart sunk. Every year, I don't like to talk about it because the effect it had on the county, the town, it was almost like sitting in a room with nobody in it. The silence was deafening. Can you imagine being in a town with children active all over the place and doing things and going here and there, because that school was the hub of the county? It did so much, like the church and to shut that down.

Lord sometimes we would just walk the streets, go downtown and look in the store windows, we knew we didn't have any money, but we had to get together with what was left here, with those children that was left here and try to keep communication. It was so devastating because of no activities. Can you imagine no school bus to ride and during that time of the year there was still none. All during the summer you couldn't do anything but just sit around and stay in the house. And even though I went to visit some, when June came, I was back home and there was nothing here in Farmville.

I can't describe it, I can't describe how I felt, it was as though I was in a different country. Because like I said, some children had no hope at all. They knew they weren't going anywhere and they didn't. It's hard to express. It's hard to explain because it affected the whole county and the town for five whole years. They hadn't made any progress, but the hope that I had was in my church because Reverend Griffin was the leader of the march and the strike and he managed to get the schools open. And every Sunday, with activities in the church, Bible schools and meetings, he kept us hopeful, but some children left, whole families moved away because their parents would not let their children go with other people so and they decided ALL OF US ARE GOING and that broke up a whole lot of families and friendships, because I never saw them again. They never returned. It was like a death, so many deaths at one time and it broke up relationships. I remember one lady saying that if she doesn't hurry and come back, she ain't going to have a husband.

After five long years of Prince Edward County's public schools being closed the U.S. Supreme Court reached a landmark decision. On May 25th 1964, Griffin v. School Board of Prince Edward County ruled that in their attempt to avoid desegregation, the county had violated the rights of their students to an education and that they could not use public funds to support private segregated schools. Most importantly the ruling ordered Prince Edward County schools to be reopened immediately. Hearing this news, many of the children were traveling back home preparing to attend school for the first time in five years. Their stories are told here:

Patricia Lee -Adams

Patricia Lee was going into third grade when school closed.

I found out that school had been closed, well at that age you really didn't understand what was going on. You know going into the third grade, you just knew that there weren't any schools. My reaction? Well, I felt that I was missing out on a lot and didn't know why.

When school closed, we walked to Lutheran Church in Lunenburg County, that was where we were the first year and that year really didn't count because it wasn't really a school. The next year we went to Lunenburg Elementary School. We stayed in Lunenburg until the end of the year and then we came back to Prince Edward; that was the year that the Free School opened, I missed.

John Augustus Baker, III

I was in the third grade when school closed. I found out about the school closing when I heard my parents talking about it. I was somewhat happy at first when I found out  but later on, I wish school was open. When the school closed, let me see, the first year I went to Centreville, Maryland. The second-year school closed, Maryville, Virginia and then the next six years I went to school in New Kent County, about 25 miles east of Richmond, Virginia. When school reopened, I was in New Kent County, Virginia through the fall of 1967. In 1968, I came back to Prince Edward. I was in the 12th grade. My father got a job in Prince Edward to teach Vocational Agriculture. Mr. Thomas Mayfield, who was the agriculture teacher, left and went to Africa. Mr. Mayfield told my father about the job and recommended him to the principal. Yea, I was at Prince Edward one year; I graduated 12th grade from R.R. Moton High School.

I am retired right now from teaching at Prince Edward County Elementary school and also as a guidance counselor there. Let me see, I think I was there--I was there all together for 41 years. I taught for eight years; fifth grade a few years; and then I did fourth grade. Then after my teaching days of teaching General Ed., I was a Guidance School Counselor at the Elementary School.

If school had not closed, I still would be teaching in school or science, something like that. I guess it was bad because a lot of people missed out on school, and we had to move a lot you know, had to meet new friends all of the time, you know? Had to make a new start, so I didn't like that so much, you know. I kind of like to stay in one place. I had to adjust to different teachers, different curriculum and things like that.

Betty Baskin Bolden

I was in the 4th grade when school closed. I found out about the school closing from my parents.

My reaction when I heard about the school closing, I was somewhat sad because I liked my teacher Mrs. Foster; I enjoyed learning and recess time. I also enjoyed planting seeds and seeing them grow.

When school closed, I went to Orange County, Virginia, Lightfoot Elementary for 1 year before Free School opened. When school reopened, I was placed in the 7th grade because of my age.

Now, I am a retired Registered Nurse, Master's Health Care Administration Enrolled in Theology classes at Global University. I volunteer in chapel ministries at the Woodlands, Centra Hospice, Trinity Mission, and (Prison) Ladies Inmates at Piedmont. If school had not closed, I would have been a Cardiologist Surgeon.

Alice Jones -Miller

I was in the 4th grade when school closed. The teachers told us about the school closing. When I heard it, I was surprised and wanted to know why they closed the schools. We went to live with our aunt and stayed with her and it allowed me and my sister to go to school in Patterson, New Jersey. When school reopened, we went to school at Mary E. Branch and I was in the 7th grade and then I went to R. R. Moton High School and graduated. After I graduated, I got married.

With grandkids now and retired now from Carbone, because you know all of the factories closed down. I just didn't do anything else. If school had not closed, I wanted to be a beautician. I would have loved to have my own bakery, because I bake cakes, pies, bread from scratch. If I had attended school, I would love to have my own salon and bakery. It didn't come around to that, so I didn't get to.

Charlie Thomas Barksdale

When school closed, I was in the 7th grade. I found out about school closing from my brother. He was older than us. He talked about marching in Farmville with Barbara Johns, my brother was there too, so that's how I found out, he told us about the school closing.

When school closed, the first year I couldn't go anywhere. I worked for my father because my father got hurt and you know my daddy owned all those pigs, cows and stuff so somebody had to feed them. I volunteered to stay home. I missed school for the first two years and then the third year

I went away to Washington D.C. and I stayed in D.C. for two years and went to a Catholic school up there, Holy Redeemer, and after that I came back home, my brother George stayed up there. Fred Evans and I, came back and the third year I went to Richmond, Virginia and I stayed with a Doctor Basset. I went to Virginia Randolph School in Richmond for two years. Everywhere I went in life, God been good to me. I can't say no more, like I say God has been really good to me. He carried me through a lot of seen and unseen dangers, carried me to Vietnam and brought me back. I had a few scratches, my wife says I am crazy (he and wife are laughing), but I am still here.

When school opened, I came back to Prince Edward, Robert R. Moton and that is where I graduated.

Well if school had not closed, I probably would have been a professional football player. Sports, I loved sports back then. When I did graduate, I got a three-year scholarship to Virginia State College, but I couldn't go, Uncle Sam said I want you first, so Ms. Harris the local board lady told me you could forget all about college son, Uncle Sam needs you, so back then they were drafting people and I didn't want to draft, so I went on and volunteered.

You know, I have never been racial with black or white because I was brought up with both, you know. Matter of fact I went to the army, I loved it. You get to know a lot of people. I see ... Puerto Ricans, all that you wouldn't get to see around here, I get to see the world, plus I carried my wife to enjoy the world with me. She went to Germany, Louisiana, and Hawaii.

George W. Barksdale

When school closed, I was in the fourth grade. I found out about the school closing by word of mouth, because we didn't attend school the next year. And then we realized that there was no school and everyone in the community was coming up with the idea of some at home training or some churches have classes.

I was very disappointed about school being closed, very disappointed because I had gotten to the point where I had some friends that I knew when I graduated from one class, that we were going to be in class together. After school was closed, they were sent away to be with relatives up north, so it was very disappointing.

When school closed, the first year I went to Washington and I stayed with the Richardson family, she was a single mother and her first name was Lillian and she had two children. She had a daughter who was in her first year of college, named Julia and she had a son who was about three years younger than myself, his name was Billy. I stayed there until I graduated, and then I came home for the summer until I went to Washington to continue my education.

The first time I stayed with the Brown's and my brother Charlie, he and myself stayed with different families and we were close and they always made sure we saw each other every weekend. The second year I was with another single mother, Mrs. Dorothy Brown, and she had a son named Billy also and there I attended a catholic school.

When they started the Free School in 1963, I had this family who wanted to accept me in Hampden, Virginia so I went to Hampden, Virginia and my brother Charlie had a family who wanted to accept him in Newport News, Virginia to continue his education. I discovered that the two families were related, they were brothers. The one I stayed with, Andrew Basset, he was a doctor and the one my brother Charlie stayed with, he was a dentist; they were black. We got a chance to see each other every other weekend. It was a blessing.

I came back here in 1964. When it first opened up Robert R. Moton High School is where I finished my last four years. I was kind of glad they let them change it to Prince Edward County Schools, because if I am not mistaken, they were trying to name it after the superintendent, so I am glad they decided to keep it.

I had one brother who was a year older than myself and he didn't' go away to school, because he was more skilled driving the tractor and helping my father around the house, he stayed here and they chose to let me go since I wasn't too handy around the house, (he laughed) I guess.

What would you have liked to have done or been if school had not closed? You know that is hard. I have thought about it a couple of times, but I look back and by me going away to school, it kinda helped me and it encouraged me to get my education. I got a chance to see the way different families live, you know other than things here at home and I think by me going away to school, kinda made me a better person, and made me what I am today. Because when I was going to school here, in Prince Edward County, before I went away to school, the Klu Klux Klan was a big thing than in the neighborhood and they, matter of fact, three or four miles up the road from where I lived, they had a field and I guess it was approximately about 30 acres and they kept the grass cut down because that was where they held their rallies and it was a frightening thing at night, you know, when you go by there, you saw 3 or 4 crosses out there burning. You can imagine how frightening it was for families to sit in their front yard and see that. I would really like to see your book come out because I want to know where, I guess it was a few years ago, I went to the school for a class reunion. I got a chance to meet some of my old classmates and we got a chance to walk around and realized how many of our classmates that were no longer here.

I am retired now, I went into the military after I graduated and then after I retired from the military, I felt a little lazy. So I decided to go to work for the department of corrections, because I had three brothers working for the department of corrections, and I stayed there for 15 years until I got injured, and then they medically retired me from the department of corrections.

Barbara Welton Harris

When school closed that was my first year, first grade. I was told by my mother about the school closing. Really, I was too young, I didn't have a reaction.

When school closed, I was home maybe one year; after a while I went to school in West Virginia. When school reopened, I was back in the state then, I came to Mary E. Branch and they placed me in the 5th grade.

I am retired from Piedmont Geriatrics Hospital, my last place of employment. I am really not, I am kind of satisfied with my life, how it turned out.

I really do think it was awful of how it went down because of the reasoning of how it went down. Because they didn't want to mix with black students, so they closed the black schools.

Ernestine Virginia Lane Harris

 I was finishing up the 7th grade and beginning the 8th. I found out about the school closing during the summer when the Board of Supervisors met and said they would not refund public schools. At first, I thought it was just a big joke and that we were just going to get a vacation for a few months. Then it got serious and I realized it was not a joke, we were not going to be able to have any public education.

When school closed the first couple years, I went nowhere but right here in Farmville, I attended the crafts programs that were given at First Baptist and Beulah AME Church and the second two years I went to Chesapeake, Virginia, Prestwood High School. When school reopened, I returned to Free School in 1964, to the public school in 1965 and graduated in 1965 from Robert Russa Moton.

I worked for ARAMARK for 34 years, the food service at Longwood University, but because of job cuts, my job, I was eliminated in January. I am actually looking for a job.

If school had not closed, I would like to have become a school teacher. I really feel that if public education had not been discontinued, that I would have graduated. Even though I graduated, I would have continued college to a four-year college, got a degree and I would have been able to teach. Even though my life has not been really, really bad, it has been successful in some ways and in other ways things that I would have like to done with my life, I could not do it because of having kids and not having the money and having to work after losing my husband in 1996.

James Edward Holcomb

 I was in the 6th grade when school closed. My parents were farmers and sharecroppers while in Virginia. I found out about the school closing by my parents. I don't remember having a reaction. I knew I wanted to go to school.

I attended Charlotte County schools for two years. I stayed with my uncle and rode with my cousins to the county line to catch the school bus. When school re-opened, I returned to Prince Edward. I was in the 8th grade. I graduated in 1968 at Robert R. Moton High School.

I am now a retired Educator. I volunteered for the military after graduating high school and served 3 years in the U.S. Army and was stationed in Vietnam for a year. I graduated from Virginia State with a Master's Degree, worked for Prince Edward Public schools for 31 years in the positions of teacher, coach, athletic director and administrator assistant to the principal. I have also been an ordained minister for 23 years.

I dreamed of being a professional baseball player. In fact, I went to a baseball camp at the University of Maryland and was chosen by the Pittsburg Pirates to compete. Out of 502 participants only 50 were chosen to move forward. I was the fastest outfielder and the 2nd fastest player of 502 athletes. I was not selected for the team because I was already in my twenties.

The closing of the schools had a negative impact on a lot of lives, but most of us did not give up. The folks of Prince Edward had a lot of stamina and fought for a better education for the children.

Jordan T. Jackson, Jr.
I had completed 2nd grade when schools closed. Would have entered 3rd grade in the fall of 1959. I learned of school closing from my parents. When I learned schools were closed, I had a muted reaction. Did not quite understand the significance at such an early age. Torn between confusion and joy that I wouldn't have to go to school.

After the school closed, we relocated to Philadelphia for 2 of the 5 years schools were closed. I did not attend school for 2 years, and attended "the Free Schools" for the final year of school closings. When school reopened, I had a much better understanding of what had occurred and was quite relieved that life was returning to some sense of normalcy. I was also developing anger over the treatment of black folk in our community.

When school re-opened, I was entering the 7th grade. I was fortunate enough to skip grades 6th and 8th which allowed me to graduate on time.

I am currently retired after 33 years with General Electric. I enjoy traveling, live music, and occasional round of golf.

Because of my age when school closed and the good fortune to have parents who valued education, the closings did not significantly affect my aspirations for the future. I was able to attend college, earn an MBA, and go to a career in business management.

In addition to the above comments, I think it is extremely important that we keep the memory of the school closings alive. Not as a source of bitterness and resentment, but as a reminder of the severe impact racial prejudice can have on human lives. Many people lost their opportunity to pursue their dreams and were permanently scarred. We must never allow this to happen again and continue to learn from this dark moment in our history

Doris Day Miller- Johnson

I was going into the 3rd or 4th grade when the school closed. We were getting ready to go to Worsham. I found about the school closing and it was just communication, it was on the television, people were talking, it just told that we were not going to school down here. When I heard that school closed, well I was a young girl, little girl. I thought to myself, well I am not going to school anymore, so where am I going to go, and what am I going to do?

When school was closed, we stayed around the house with my mother, helped with the chores, and my sister Clara Miller was in Brooklyn at the time and she suggested to my mom to send me to go to school in Brooklyn so I went to Brooklyn, went to PX133, I started in the 3rd grade in Brooklyn, New York. I came home when school reopened and started school at Worsham Elementary. I went to Robert Russell Moton High School and it turned into Prince Edward County High where I graduated in 1972. Now I am fortunate to still have a job and to be employed. I work at Powhatan Correctional Center for men; I am a security officer. I went to Mary E. Branch II and when I completed, I think 6th or 7th grade, and then I went to the high school and went to the 8th grade.

If school had not closed, I had always looked to being a school teacher, but who knows what the opportunity was, things change so, to tell you the truth, there was an opportunity right there, bad one, that occurred, but it either made you strong or made you weak, so I am glad, Jesus, it made me strong. What I would like to say about the school closing? "It was wrong!

James Randall (Mike)

I was in the second grade when school closed in 1959. I found out about the school closing from my parents. I felt I had to find somewhere to go to school. I left with my uncle Big Boy when he was down here and moved to Manhattan, New York and went to school. When school reopened here in Prince Edward County, I was in the seventh grade, I returned home and continued going to school here. I left school and went into the Job Corp when I was 17 years old. I attended Essex Community College in Newark, New Jersey and took up Business Administration. I also took up key punching at a job training center. I am now retired from Mcquire VA Hospital 22 years and convalescing from a stroke. If school had not closed, my dream was to go to Virginia State or Norfolk State that is what I wanted to do.

I think it was a shame that school closed and kids couldn't continue their education on the level that they were on and had to go through a long drought without being in school.

Rebecca Randolph

When the schools closed in 1959, I was in the 7th grade. I

did not attend public schools for two years. After the 3rd year our parents met with the Lunenburg school system administration to get us registered in school. We entered the school system in Lunenburg County Public Schools. There I stayed until schools opened in Prince Edward County Public Schools.

There I stayed until schools opened in Prince Edward County Free Schools in the 1963-64 school year.

My two sisters and brother and other neighborhood students had to find a way to meet the Lunenburg bus. We walked across the county line to meet that bus. While being in Lunenburg County Schools it was a pleasant stay. I met and still remain a part of a class reunion with many classmates. My older sister while attending Lunenburg graduated from that school in 1963. Coming back to Prince Edward County when schools reopened, my brother graduated from the Free School in 1964. That left my younger sister and I to stay and graduate in Prince Edward Public Schools in 1966 and 1967.

After graduation in 1966, I attended a Skill Center in Crewe, Va. and received a degree in Clerk Typist. I always like secretarial work. In 1970, I came back to Prince Edward County School System to work as an accounts payable bookkeeper and work for 42 years before retiring in 2012. In 2009, I received a Bachelor of Science Degree in Business Administration from Saint Paul's College in Lawrenceville, Virginia with the help of a Brown Scholarship. I am happy that Saint Paul's College stepped up to be a pattern to other colleges to help the students of Prince Edward and other counties in Virginia and enable all of the students to be college students and to bring us to where we are today.

At this stage in my life at my age I was very proud to be the first in my family to get a 4-year college degree.

Ruth Lee-Taylor

I was in the 5th grade going into the 6th when school closed. I found out that school had closed from my mother. When I heard that school had closed, at that time I believe I felt surprised, confused, really, I didn't know what was going on. Closing the schools? That was very devastating. I didn't know how and what to think.

When school closed the first couple years I stayed at home, and I and some others had classes in the basement of the Miller Building, the basement of the Methodist Church and I believe First Baptist. It's been such a long time. I believe we did classes there for several weeks and then my sister Phyllis and I went to Springfield, Massachusetts and stayed with foster parents. The first couple we stayed with; their names were Lawson, they were an older couple, we stayed with them a couple of weeks. Then we were moved to another couple who had a daughter our age, their name was Samuels and we stayed until the year had ended. The next year I went to New Bethel Massachusetts and stayed with the Duarte family, they had five girls and my sister stayed with another family, their name was Lopes. My sister and I did not stay with the same family, she and Brenda Smith stayed together. The last year I stayed with Mr. & Mrs. Duarte, she passed a couple of years ago, she was about 84, but I went to see her in 2009, she was getting a little senile, but she knew me. When school reopened, I was in the 9th grade; I went to R.R. Moton High School and graduated.

I am now retired from 20 years of corrections, and trying to enjoy life, every minute of it. If school had not closed, I would have like to...I really don't think about it that much... going back about thinking about what I could have done. When I was young, but I used to say I wanted to be a secretary, but I don't think about it now.

The school closing was a disappointing thing. I do believe I missed out on a lot. I probably could have done better in life; better job opportunities, could have probably come my way, but I thank God I was able to retire from my job. I had and got good benefits and stuff. It was a challenge, but thank God, I made it through. Got married and raised a family and they are doing well and got grandkids.

John Toney

I stayed home when school was closed, but I did lots of things inside the home--read comic books and experimented with things.

All of my brothers and sisters stayed at home. Some of them got jobs and one of them just stayed home. I could read in the first grade because my sisters taught me how to read, they taught me how to spell and read properly. I was proud when school opened, because I could get some education, open my mind and we could learn. When I was in school, I used to make the honor roll. I got a permit from teacher, Mr. Moore because I was working at Buffalo Shook, a sawmill place at night from four to twelve, so, when I went to school, I had study hall so I would have time to study for the rest of the day. I ended up getting my GED.

Betty Jean Ward-Berryman

I was finishing the seventh grade when school closed. I found out about the school closing when one day we were at Mary E. Branch School playing during the summer and this white man came up and put the chains on the school door and told us we had to get off the school grounds because school was going to be closed. When I came home, I was telling my father about it and it was on the news. When I first heard about it, my father said they are not going to close those schools, schools will be open in September. So, I really didn't think nothing of it, but then as time got closer to September, my dad said well, they are really not going to open these schools up. I was upset. I said what are we going to do?

I went to live with my grandparents in Nottoway County, in Virginia and went to school down there. I stayed with them during the week and during the weekends I came home. I stayed with them until September 63. I went to Foster High School in Nottoway County for four years and at the beginning of 63, I came back to the free school (in Prince Edward County). I was in the 12th grade when school reopened. I graduated from the free school; there were twenty-three graduates and I was one of those 23. I am retired now, a retired teacher for 32 years. I always wanted to be a teacher and I didn't miss any time from school so I was able to accomplish that goal.

My sister and brother had to leave home. They went to Kittrell Junior College in North Carolina and my brother graduated because he was a senior. Then my sister, when the Quakers came and sent students to different places, she went to Yellow Springs, Ohio to live with a white family. My oldest brother was in college at the time.

It was just something that I never would have thought something like this would have happened in the United States of America. It is something that you will never forget. A lot of people were hurt by it and a lot of people don't want to talk about it now; an emotional thing, I guess. It is hard to even express how I feel about it; you want to hate and then you say you want to forgive and then you want to forget. Like I said some people will never forget it. Some good things came out of it, people who would not have gotten the opportunity to accomplish what they did, if school had not closed. We have come a little way, I guess (laugh). We still got a long way to go.

Doris Williams-Berryman

Doris Williams was in the seventh grade when school

closed. She said with the knowledge of the school closing, I was happy--time to have fun. After about 3 months, summer over, time for school to start, sadness set in. l always liked school, and now I start thinking what's next?

When school closed, I attended Mrs. Flossie White School Center in my community. During the fall of 1960 I went to live with my brother and family in New York for my 8th grade. I came home for the summer and was selected to move to Blacksburg, Virginia to attend school in my 9th and 10th grades. That was very challenging and successful. My parents were very supportive and encouraging. They knew I was capable of adjusting wherever I was placed.

When school reopened, I was in the 11th grade. I was very happy to be back home, and back to my familiar community and school environment.

Now I am working for the state in the department of Behavior Science.

If school had not closed, I would have gone off to college and studied Business/Psychology. I am thankful for the experience I gained from meeting people of all cultures and learning what life had to offer.

Everett Berryman, Jr.

 When school closed in 1959, I was in the 6th grade going to the 7th grade that next fall. I found out about the school closing through my parents. When I heard that schools were closed, initially it didn't take effect, I thought in general that we were going to have an extended summer vacation and school would probably reopen during the first semester. When school reopened, I attended the centers which were in Pamplin, and Prospect, Virginia (the Pamplin Center and the Prospect Center) for the first two years and the last two years I attended Carver Price High School in Appomattox County, Virginia. Initially we started commuting to my aunt and uncle's house that was across county lines, then we had to eventually move into Appomattox County. When school reopened, we moved back to Prince Edward County and attended the Free School in the school year 63-64. I was in the 9th grade.

I graduated from Robert R. Moton High School in the class of 67'. Right now, I am working in the field of Christian Education and that is pretty much what I am doing right at the moment. I am pretty much doing what I set out, exactly what I was going to do, I believe. The interruption of school just delayed it two years, but it didn't delay my ambition of who I wanted to be. Coming through high school into the military and into college and eventually the field of Christian Education and becoming a clergy and pastoring and now I am still in that field even though I did retire from Ericson General Electric.

The school closing really gave me an opportunity to find out who I was as an individual and when I tapped into who I was as an individual, it really opened up doors to what I wanted to do in order to get my education. The ideas I had and enthusiasm didn't really develop to push me on to do what I wanted to do in order to reach that point.

Shirley Jackson-Brown

I was in the first grade, promoted to the second grade when

school was closed. I found out that school was closed through my mother, Nancy Jackson. When I heard that school was closed, as a child you would say, I didn't believe it; I cried. The very first day school was to open, I went up the street and I looked at the school. I went up there to see if school was really closed. When I got there, I saw a bunch of chains on the doors and I was like changed from there as far as school was concerned.

After school closed, the first year we did nothing but the second year they had something you called schools in the basement of the church. I went to Beulah A.M. E. Church and First Baptist Church down on Main Street in Farmville for school. The second year, I went to Charlotte County. I went to live with my sister, Mary Ghee and her husband Franklin Ghee. I was in the 2nd grade. My sister and her husband had three other children in the house and they took four of us in to go to school there. Three of my siblings went to school in Charlotte County one year, and I had an older sister that was in a higher grade than we were, she kept going to school after we left there, because my sister couldn't afford all four of us in her house with her with her three children. It was too much; she couldn't handle it. So, we had to come back to Farmville the next year, but we did finish the school year out.

When school reopened, I went to the Free School, I was in the 4th grade. I was so happy to go to school. I came in full force; I was so happy. We were early, we got up early, we were really ready to go to school. My sisters and brothers were ready to go back to school. When school reopened, they put me in the fourth grade. We went by age groups, they couldn't put you in by grades, because a lot of kids hadn't been to school at all, some of them was older than I was and they were in lower grades too. It was awful, it was terrible. I never will forget that, it was awful. Great big tall boys, 6 ft tall in the 4th grade and they were older than I, it was awful. It was terrible, I thought it was awful. They took us by age, not by grades until they found out what you knew. It was like that for some years, I can't remember how many years it stayed like that, but I guess when they took up public schools, when Free School was over that is when they went to promotional. I dropped out of school as a sophomore and got my GED.

If school had not closed, I would like to had done music, teach, public relations, sing. Something good comes out of a lot of things, something bad comes out sometimes, but as for this story, the way I see it, it's some good came out of it and some bad came out of it. But it was so tragic, it was tragic because a lot of kids never ever got to go to school at all because the age they were. And they were embarrassed, they were embarrassed because they were so old and they never got a chance to go back to school. That's the part I look at and I see some of them. (she started tearing up), oh I hate talking about it. I hate talking about it. I am kind of semi-retired right now.

The hurting part is the way kids look at school now, they don't look at it as pride, honor, they don't care if they don't go, some of them, they treat the teachers awful. If I could just flick the time back and let them see how it was for even us. It was worse for our parents. Even us, let them see what we had to go through, What Barbara Johns and them had to go through, even Barbara probably had a sort of well to do family, it was some poor children back then that didn't have.

I cried for everything, I cried for my mama struggling anyway, working doing a days' work, and she got, I call it promoted to working at Longwood College, Slater, the food service back then. I thought about everything during that time, it wasn't only school closing, we had a lot of stuff to deal with. Kids these days got the bus stop in front of their houses and it picks them up, we had to walk to get on the bus, which was nothing to us, we had fun walking and playing with our friends in the morning time and some kids lived in the country and they had to walk dirt roads and get on another road, and another road, and another road until they got here.

I hated the school closing. It was very unjust. People will never understand what we went through.

Freddie Cobbs

 I had completed the 8th grade when schools closed in Prince Edward County in 1959. I really can't remember exactly how I heard about the closing. I suppose that I heard it from other people in the community. When I first heard that the schools were closed, I was excited; however, I did not think that they would be closed for five years. I just thought that they would be closed for just a short period of time.

After the schools were closed, I stayed home and helped my father on the farm. The third year, my parents allowed me to go to Arlington, Virginia. I stayed with Ernest and Mignon Johnson. He was the Supervisor of Recreation for Arlington County and his wife was a Counselor in the Washington, DC School System. During the 9th and 10th grades, I went to school at Hoffman-Boston Junior Senior High School.

When school reopened, I went to the Free Schools and completed my junior year. I graduated from Prince Edward County High School in 1965. I graduated from Virginia State College in Petersburg, Virginia in 1971 with a B.S. Degree in Electronics Technology.

My first job was an Industrial Engineer with the General Electric Company in Lynchburg, Virginia. I worked there for ten years; and after being laid off, I was hired by Stackpole Corporation as their first Black Manufacturing Engineer in 1981. They transferred me to the Headquarters in Raleigh, North Carolina in 1985. Stackpole was purchased by Ark-les Corporation in 1986 and I worked for them until 2003 when all manufacturing was moved to Juarez, Mexico. I started driving the school bus for Wake County in 2004, and I just retired on July 1, 2015.

I never knew what I wanted to do when I grew up; however; I always wanted a job that paid well so that I could earn a decent living. That is why I chose to major in Engineering.

I think that the school closing was a very sad situation and it affected so many lives and it will affect their children for generations to come because many of them never got the opportunity to finish high school. I was glad that I was able to continue even though I lost two years of school. I am glad that God allowed me to complete my education and have a good career. My wife, Pattie and I have had a wonderful life together.

Linda Edwards - Edmonds

I was 10 years old when school closed. I don't really remember how I found out that school was closed, all I know is that it came up and we didn't go the next year. When I heard that school closed - to me at 10 years old, it's not what it is now, that I would have realized it, for a child it would be unusual not to go to school the following year.

When school closed, I went to Ms. Flossie Hudson's basement. We rode on the back of Mr. Anthony Jones truck. They would pick us up and we would sit on benches on his truck and go over to her basement and have school. I went to Hampton, Virginia but it wasn't until I was out three of the four years and it was almost in the middle semester of the fourth year. When I went there, I was in the fifth grade. When school reopened, I came back in the fall semester and they promoted me here to the 7th grade at free school and then I went to the high school. I skipped the 8th grade and went to the 9th grade and graduated at the age of 17 from RR. Moton High School. In July I was 18 years old.

I am satisfied with my life, even though it might have been intended to ruin or to hold me back, but I don't feel like I was. I think this is the life I was supposed to live. All of that, that went on back there, I think every day we live is predestined. Every day of my life I feel this is what the Lord had planned for me. I think it was intended for schools to close. I think it was intended for us to be placed; I think, every day of my life I feel like this is what the lord had planned for me. I am not hostile, bitter, they didn't win, they didn't win.

I am a retired retail salesperson. If school had not closed, I think I could have been a lot of different things. I'm interested in decorating, design and stuff like that. I'm interested in fashion which I did do at Belk. If I were a man, I would be a painter. (laugh) I like to paint.

I am satisfied with my life. I feel that I am fairly educated even though I'm not a college graduate, even though I knew the possibilities that I could have done more, even though I didn't realize my potential when I was in school. But I do now. I do now. But I'm not angry with anyone about that, I know that's the way our lives were supposed to be, for a purpose, and one of them was for forgiveness. Sometimes you are put to a test to see if you could pass it and in order to pass, you have to forgive and forget. We got to forgive those people. They are dead and gone. These people around here now, their children or whatever, half of them don't even know anything about it. You have to forgive and forget. I am not hostile; I am not bitter. Every day of my life I feel this is what the lord had planned for me and I know that that is the life I was supposed to live.

Carl Eggleston

I was in the second grade promoted to the third when school closed. I found out about the school closing by my parents. We didn't have to go to school no more was my reaction. Two years I didn't go to school at all, probably went down to First Baptist Church where they had something like I consider, like a year-round vacation Bible School. The second two years my parents rented a home over in

Cumberland County, so I went there for two years at Robert Russa Moton School on route 638, they used to call it R.R. Moton then. When school reopened, we moved back. They cancelled out on the house we rented and moved back to the house we owned in Farmville. I was in the 5th grade when school reopened. I went to the Mary E. Branch II School.

I am in the Funeral business.

If school had not closed, I would like to have been doing the same thing.

Well, I think a lot of progress has been made, but a lot has yet to be done. The school I understand they're on the verge of that. I think it set the whole process back, it set everybody back.

I have written my thoughts in a number of Letters to the Editor. I also have a book of my own: *Joy and Pain, My Way,* that I hope to publish in 2020 about my experience and life now. In addition, I am grateful to Rita Odom Mosley for persevering with this project and compiling this historic book.

Carolyn Hendricks

I was in the 4th grade when school closed. My parents told me about the school closing.

I was surprised/confused. I wondered where I was going to school.

After school closed, my parents took me to live with my grandparents who lived in Pamplin, VA. I went to school in Charlotte Court House, VA. When school re-opened my parents bought me back home to go to R.R. Moton High

School. I was in the 8th grade. I finished at R.R. Moton in 1968.

I am retired now from the Department of Agriculture after 35 years of service. If school had not closed, I would have like to work for a computer company as a computer programmer.

It was a terrible thing to have happened to our community to deny us an education. A lot of children lost out in getting an education. Their family couldn't afford to send them out of state nor had relatives in other counties to go live with.

Throughout the five years public schools were closed, many of the children were working and many were cleaning white family homes, taking care of their children, and working on their farms and tobacco fields. A child labor workforce was starting as early as the age of 12. The author was one of them for a very short while.

Janie Gee Walton

I was in the 6th grade when school closed. I found out about school being closed by my parents. I stayed home. There were nine children in our family and my parents could not afford to send us anywhere else. When school closed, I had to go to work as a child. I was the oldest of 9 children and two of my siblings were visually impaired. My father suffered from war injuries, but he did sawmill work and farming. I was very sad because I did not understand why it was happening.

When school re-opened, we returned to Prince Edward County. I had dreams of doing things like any child however, because of the circumstances; I had to work to help with the family. I really wanted to finish school. I missed out on a lot. I missed out on things that can never be replaced. I am now retired.

Moses Scott

 I was in the 9th grade when school closed in 1959. I found out about the school closing by radio. I can even remember the announcer, Al Smith and he essentially said that the public schools will not be opening in September. When I heard that school was closed, we didn't think it would really be closed, we thought it would be delayed. Of course, it turned out to be much, much more than a delay. Certainly, it was an extension of summer vacation so that was good news to a kid.

Initially I didn't go anywhere; I missed a year out of school. I worked cleaning houses, I also worked cleaning the private school they were putting together, was developing for the white kids. I worked washing the windows so they would have a nice clean place to work, but it was a job.

When school reopened, I wasn't there when school reopened, I missed one year, I left the following year and did not come back. The American Friends Service came to Farmville, sometime probably in the winter time, March, had a meeting at Farmville, my mom attended and essentially, they had canvased the country and found families who were willing to keep the Black children as foster children, quote on quote, so that they could continue their education. And my mom came home and she said Moses, these people from up North came down and they said they had families who would keep you so you could go back to school. Mama said Moses, do you want to go? I knew nothing, I had never been out of Prospect, Virginia to my knowledge and I said yes mam. The Quakers put all of us on a Grey Hound bus, it was 6 of us from Prince Edward County, the Hendricks, the Cobbs, seven of us in all was placed in Moorestown, New Jersey, which is about 10 miles from Camden, and so they met us at the Grey Hound bus station, took us over to Moorestown. I was the first stop, it was 612 Church Street and Rick Holler who was the Quaker, who was supervisor or manager, he knocked on the door, this lady, Mrs. Mattie Morgan came to the door, opened the door and smiled and said Moses your room is upstairs. I stayed with them two years and I worked and they accepted me as part of the family and I did some tasks, but they knew my job was to study and Mrs. Morgan used to say Moses up patting his feet at night so he didn't go to sleep while he was studying, of course I had to do that and you know I did pretty well. I went to Moorestown High. That was the first stop.

After that, the next stop was Boston, Massachusetts. During the summer before the Quakers had asked me, did I want to go to Europe with them, they were taking high school students to Europe to promote peace and brotherhood. I said I never been on a plane, I said mama what should I do? She said that's a good opportunity and the plane is safe, and so I went there. I stayed in Europe, I got there around June, July, if remember correctly, stayed a couple months, started in Zurich, Switzerland, Germany, Czechoslovakia, Soviet Union, Russia, Moscow, then Germany, came home, but when I got back home school wise, I found out that I wasn't going back to Moorestown. They said that Moorestown system can't support the kids from Prince Edward County, so we found a home for you in Boston.

I got on a grey hound bus, went up to Boston, and this little man met me at the bus station. I was 6 feet three then, 185-190, and he said my name is Dr. Pitso Pensor, he was from

Poland, one of the places I had been and he also had been in Australia, one of the places I visited before and we stayed with Dr. Pensor and his family, three kids and his wife the year to finish high school. I went to Newton High School in Newton Massachusetts, right outside of Boston. In fact, they were so kind, they got out of the master bedroom, gave me the master bedroom and they went to a smaller room and so I've had so much help and so much support and it is ironic that I am in a business that helps people, that's what we do in home health aides, helping people to enjoy a better quality of life, so that was a great experience.

I own Right At Home. Right at Home is part or a national franchise and my company covers Essex County in New Jersey. We have some great aides; the aides are the heart and soul of the business. I don't do anything; they make us look really, really great.

If school had not closed, what I would have done? – I don't know, I don't know, you know for me it was taking a lemon and making lemonade. I was happy, but one reason I wanted to do real well, just to show white people that Black people could excel and everything that I have done from that point on supports that, going to college, going to business school and I go, not so much, it was a great school but I wanted to go to the toughest school to show them that Black people can excel. The main thing is, I probably would have done better than I did, if it hadn't closed, but that's just me, it's all the other people that I feel for, people who wasn't as fortunate, and there were people much smarter than I was, you know I can think of them, I could see them and they had so much to offer and because of that they weren't able to offer everything that they could have offered, so I think something should be done about it, something should be done about it, the story is not over yet.

Leroy Ross

 I was passing to the third grade when school closed. I think my mama told me that we weren't going to school the next year. That young, when I heard about it, I just thought that I had some free time in the beginning.

When the school closed, I worked on my grandfather's farm. When school reopened, I went back and when I starting realizing what was going on, I still graduated on time. I was the last class of R.R. Moton. If school had not closed I probably would have done the same thing as I did, basically when I started going to the centers in Farmville with Reverend Griffin, you know I got a sense of what civil rights and everything was meaning, so me and Reverend Griffin worked very close together. Yea, and even though a lot of people didn't realize that among other things, but he called me in and said, "I want you to go in and lead these um protest or whatever from the students. A lot of people wanted the glory; I just wanted to do the things that was right for black people.

Right now, I am working for a courier company that delivers medicine and stuff to nursing homes, but I still coach softball, which for a long time my softball coaching dealt with the guys I grew up with from Farmville and we were a very tough team, you know.

The only thing I could say about the closing of the schools was that it was a prejudice act, you know and the folks of Prince Edward County that were the powers to be at that time didn't want integration. So rather than to integrate, they decided to close the schools. They didn't care anything about us and one of the main things is that when I was living out on the farm I use to work for this guy and when I was going up to his farm to work every day, his kids were down there catching the bus to go to school. The other part to that and I didn't realize it until later, he was on the Prince Edward County School Board and that really upset me. Because I was saying that he was one of the people that I went to work for everyday that was keeping me out of school. But it also made me think that no matter what you try to do to me, I'm going to make it and that's why I was glad I graduated on time, graduated 5th in my class, so those are the things that drove me and my mentor Reverend Griffin. He kept me on the straight and narrow and a lot of things that he was trying to tell me, I might not have realized all of them at the time, but they came to fruition through the years.

Alda Doreatha Morton-Booth

Alda Morton was being promoted to the fourth grade when school "closed. My parents told me that we could not go back to school that coming up year because white people did not want us in the school with them and we felt very, very bad. It was five of us, so what we did after they told us that we couldn't go back to school - so during the summer we went to different people and work on the farm helping with tobacco and some of us made $7.00 a day, some of us worked in the hay fields, but we made it. That's how we made our living until the schools reopened.

It was too many of us and my parents couldn't afford to send us anywhere, so we had to stay at home while school was closed. In the summer time when the white people came from up north, we did go to school in Darlington Heights, Virginia. They taught us reading and math and they gave us a snack and several of us went there. We really did enjoy that. We went to Tracy Spencer Post, Tracy Spencer, owned the VFW post he had a little building we went to and had school there, like a little church building.

When school was opened, we went back to school, we were glad, we went back to school the first day and attended school every day until I graduated in 1969 from Robert Russell High School in Prince Edward County.

Now I am a Para Professional at the Middle School Prince Edward County Public School.

If school had not closed, I would have been a registered nurse like my Aunt Etta Lee was. That's what I always wanted to be, my goal to be a registered nurse like Aunt Etta Lee. I say it was very, very frustrating, but we were brought up to be kind and nice. We didn't fight. We were very angry, but we never got in any fights about it and we always felt bad when we saw white people because we figure they didn't like us. If they looked at us a certain way, we say, they don't like us and some of us even spoke, but they never spoke.

We would ask mom and dad, why they don't speak to us and they would tell us maybe they didn't hear us to make us feel good, but we went through a lot. It was very emotional because a lot of us will not come back because they said that they were too old to come back.

So, in 2005, when they pardoned us, the governor. Then they told us that they were going to give us money to go back to college, a lot of us went back, but a lot of us didn't because they thought they was still too old. I took advantage of it and I went. I worked at day time at Stackpole Components Company, sometimes ten hours, twelve hours whatever, I went to school at night at the Mary E. Branch which is the Moton Museum now and I got my classes there.

I graduated in 2009 and I was very, very happy. I have a BS Degree from Saint Paul's College in Lawrenceville, Virginia. Thanks to them. So, I am very happy.

David Miller

 I was in the fourth grade when school closed. I got out of school one day and my mother told me the next day that there is no more school. School was closing because of racist, black and white and stuff like that. When I heard that school was closed, I felt bad because I wanted to get an education, and make something of my life. I always said when I grow up, I will take care of my mother. When I was 9 years old, I use to go up to the golf field in Farmville and caddy all day long and some days they would give me $1.50 and if I get lucky, they would give me $2.00. After that my father told me that the man wants me to come and work in the tobacco field. I said I didn't know anything about tobacco, and he said the only thing you do is when the mule come, take the tobacco and put it on the mule cart as the mule pulled it up the field.

The ladies would twist and tie it on the stick and load it and they take it to the barn, and we would have to fill the barn before we got paid. We didn't get paid by the hour or nothing like that. Every time we filled a barn, we got $5.00, some days we do one because the barn is so big, then another day we fill two barns and we get paid $10.00. Every time I got some money, I take it home and give it to my mother. I never kept anything, I used to walk around with sneakers on with holes in the shoes. I would just take a piece of card board and put it in the sneakers. Every time I got a nickel or dime or something like that, I would take it home and give it to my mother. I have been blessed.

My sister Marie came down from California to stay with us; she was on a week vacation. They were sitting around and I asked my mother and father could I pack up and go to California, because I want my education. My mother said, "You want to go that far? ... You would be a long way from us;" and I said yea, I want to learn something. I packed my clothes and went to California. I stayed out there seven years. The part that hurt me real bad, when I found that my father died ... and we were just getting to California, so my sister and her husband told me that financially we don't have the money to send you right back to Virginia to the funeral. So, I said to myself, I am going to school and try to learn all I can; and my brother said, I am going to take you to Edgewood Inn. It was the only hotel out there and he said, I am going to teach you how to be a bus boy, wash dishes, mop the floor, anything to make some money.

Every penny I made I asked my sister and brother in law; did they want anything and they said no. I opened me an account and put it in the bank and I saved every penny until I got enough money. I came back to Virginia from California when they told me school was opened. I was in the 11th grade, so I told my mother I wanted to get my education, when she asked me do you want to go to school. I came back, I had my papers and everything, I went to R.R. Moton High School in Farmville; they took my name and the papers I had, so they signed me up. I was supposed to graduate in the 12th grade and they told me I would get my diploma. At the time when graduation was coming, I had to leave because my brother got sick in New York, so I went to New York to help him and his family.

I retired, after working in New York for 22 years in the garment center. After 20 years, you can retire, so I went over that. From there I went to Jersey. I worked for the company, DC, for twenty-three years, New England Freight Company. One day I got sick and they told me they would put me in early retirement. But when it was time for me to retire, they had to run me away, because I am a work-a-holic. The Scope Center in Farmville heard that I like to dance, so they asked me, do you think you can come to volunteer at scope and teach the senior citizens how to dance and exercise? I said yes, it would give me something to do. On Mondays I went to the Farmville Scope Center; Wednesdays, I go to Prospect, where there are a little younger senior citizens, and teach them exercise and the electric slide;, and Thursdays I go to Charlotte Court House, where the older senior citizens are, 70, 80, 90 years old and one who is 104. When I leave people they have a smile on their face. I have been blessed; God has been good to me.

If school had not closed, I would like to have been for my mother and father to be proud of me. I had seven brothers and seven sisters. My mother used to work for these people to clean the house and all of that. My dream was someday I wanted to take care of my mother, let her take it easy. She used to bring shoes home and everybody tried the shoes on and when they got to me, I said yea, I could wear the shoes. The shoes were hurting my feet so bad, I didn't want to throw them away. I used to walk around with shoes and sneakers on with holes in them and I use to take cardboard and put in them. I said to myself, I don't want my mother to be doing this. I want to go and get some money and take care of her because she works hard enough to take care of us. Sometime I wish I never left Virginia, but my belief is that God knows your future. He knew what happens to me that is the reason I went through what I went through. I am not regretting it, because I know He is the Greatest God in the world, without Him we wouldn't be anything.

Frank Harrison

I was in the ninth grade when school closed. I found out about school closing from people in the community and hearing it from the radio.

When I heard school had closed, I was very surprised and knowing my family situation, with the farm, I felt like it might be the end of my schooling. I knew my grandfather was not going to send my brother and me anywhere away from the farm to continue our schooling. My grandmother had just passed away the month before school was supposed to reopen. She would have made some kind of arrangement to send us somewhere. My grandfather just didn't know the importance of an education. He would send my brother and me to the white farmers to work in the fields on school days and the white farmers kept their children in school. I didn't know that at the time, but as I grew older, I could see the picture in full color.

My grandfather kept us home until he became very sick and we stopped raising some of the major crops. When I became 18 years of age, I got a public job and the farm finally became a large garden. My grandfather was eventually put in a hospital in Maryland State and after his stay there, he stayed with one of his daughters for a year or so, finally passed away. I went to stay with my brother (older brother) here in the area.

When school reopened, I continued public work, I did not return to school. I retired and I'm still raising gardens and helping people here and there.

As a young teenager, I didn't have much of a vision for my future because growing up on the farm, I had work looking me in the face from every direction, not giving me time to think about anything else. I went to military in 1965 and received an assignment that put me aboard a navy ship (USS AMERICA CVA-66) an aircraft carrier for two years, where I had an opportunity to enter into a study program in which I received my GED equivalent. The GED equivalent was my requirement to get a job on the N & W Railroad in Crewe, Virginia, where I worked for 35 ½ years before retiring in 2005. I really enjoyed what I was doing and I wouldn't have wanted it any other way. (As far as what I would have wanted to do)

To the children of the world, the parents of the community, the public officials at every level all the way to the President of the United States, I think education is at its most importance today than ever before. With the technology of today and the speed at which it is changing, a number of people that has been shut out of the workforce because the lack of Education. I hope the reading of this story be more encouraging and what it means to have an education and the importance of it. Keep the school doors open!

John H. Evans

 When school closed, I had passed to the 8th grade. I heard about the school closing on TV news. I worked on the farm; I didn't go anywhere. I went to school in Charlotte County Schools. When school reopened, I was happy to return home and go to school. At that

time, I was not sure what I would have done if school had not closed.

I am owner of my own business.

Stanley Johnson

 I was in the third grade, so I was about 10, 11 years old I guess when school closed. I found out about the school closing because I was in it. When I heard it, I was destroyed, I mean, you know because we needed our education. Yes, I was really struck hard, because I knew that I was going to need an education and my parents were telling me that I was going to need an education so when school closed down that was kind of a shock to me, because I really didn't know what was happening. Well, when school closed my parents were a little too poor to send me away to go to the other schools like the other kids in the neighborhood went away, so I went away with some friends and worked on a farm in Appomattox, Virginia during the time school was off.

When school reopened, I went back to school, I went back, graduated in 1970 and I went into service, after that I just you know, continued life on, started serving the Lord and trusting in him and everything seem to work out pretty good.

If school had not closed, oh, man I could have been - you know, I always wanted to manage something, some kind of office, I don't know, some kind of job where you know you could walk around with a shirt and tie on. I always wanted that type of job, but because of my education it isn't like it's supposed to be, you know, it cut me back a little bit, but it didn't hurt me cause I know God got me.

I'm retired now. I stayed in service for 2 years and after I got out of service I went to work. I worked up in Lynchburg Foundry for 27 ½ years and then I opened up a carpet and house cleaning business on my own. Well the closing of the school, I hope that everybody learns something, you know, I mean it was a bad incident, but now we got to start moving forward. We just can't let that really hinder us now, because we got kids coming up and we don't want them to take the hatred or nothing we don't want them to be like that. We want them to be able to live and work together and be a one nation under God.

In the fall of 1964 about 1,500 students, (all but eight were black), attend classes in the Prince Edward County public schools for the first time in five years. You will hear the story of two of the White children whom attended.

Richard (Dickie) Moss

My father, Dr. C. Gordan Moss' first teaching job after college was the Episcopal High School, a private boarding school in Alexandria, Virginia.

He had pre-enrolled me to start there in the 8th grade. The summer of the Prince Edward School closing in 1959 was the end of my 7th grade year at the white Farmville Elementary School. Instead of going to High, I went to the Saint Christopher Episcopal Boarding School in Richmond, Virginia. When the public schools reopened in the summer of 1963 under the Kennedy administration, I was going into my senior year that fall.

My father asked me if I would be willing to go to the, what was called at that time the Free School so I could prove that integration wasn't the end of the world like people back then seemed to think it would be. I quickly told him I would and it was based mainly on the social and economic troubles he had because of standing up for reopening the public schools the past four or five years. He lost most of his friends and almost lost his teaching job at Longwood. The governor of state had to step in. He said they won't because a college professor has a right of free speech, so I went there mainly for him. There is a *Time Magazine* Article in September of 1963 that tells that story called, "My Decision."

When I went there, he said you are gonna learn a lot about people and he was right and I enjoyed the year. The kids were very friendly to me. It had a good impact on my life.

I am retired, I taught for 35 years in a high school at Columbia, South Carolina, inter-city schools. I retired 5 years ago.

Betty Jo Lewis

I started out when I was six years old at Worsham, when it was an all-white school, ok, I rode the L.L. Irving bus. Then we moved, when we moved, I was in second grade and I went to Green Bay, Virginia Elementary School and it was an all-white school too. Now when the school closed, I didn't go to school anywhere. I was 7 when I got out of school going on 8 that July, when school closed, but I was out until I was 13, and didn't' go to school anywhere. When I went back to school in the 3rd grade, it was all-Black school in Worsham, the white school had left there, I don't know what happened there, it was all-white school when I started there, I don't know all the history of that, but me and my brother got off the bus there and we were in the paper at Worsham at the all Black school and I stayed there until I went to R.R. Moton High School.

God bless every last one of you. You all were excellent to us; I love every last one of you. It was a lot of you and they meant a lot to me. They could have been cruel to us, but we could not say that about any of you. All teachers, all children, we had best friends with them. I was a child, but my daddy did not believe in segregated schools. They had been good to us and we lived with them all of our life. We worked with them and went to school with them and I don't regret a bit of it. I'm not ashamed of where I went to school.

People back in those days looked down on Black people so bad, I actually felt sorry for them. It was so wrong. I told anybody who said something about Black people, I tell them their blood is red just like mine. You know God made everybody. I look back when we went to school there, they looked at us like we were stupid because we were going to that school, these were white people, not black people. We went to an all-Black church, yes, we did, and you know that I was not shamed of it.

Some parents sacrificed so much so their kids could go to an all-white school, rather than to accept it. Some of the white didn't go, most of the whites in Farmville went over there and supported Academy School and the parents put them over there so they wouldn't have to mix like we did. They are still paying fees to go to that school, now what do they do, they humble themselves. They are doing what they should have done way back in the 50's and put their kids right in there with us. When they got out of the Academy school, what were they going to do, stay separated all their lives and now look what's happening, Black and White are working together and also marrying. My, have the time changed.

Unfortunately, not everyone returned to Prince Edward County. Some had already graduated, started their own family or stayed in the school where they had relocated. This was particularly true for those that were close to graduating. Parents that were forced to move their entire families had by this time made a home for their children in other places. Many had permanently joined the workforce, gotten married or entered into the military. It was very sad not see your best friend or classmates in school with you. A great deal of them never returned.

Lester Thornton

I was going to the eighth grade when school closed. I found out about the school closing; well it was a lot of conversation about it. A lot of concerns, my mother and father, they talked about it a lot. When I heard it, well my reaction blended into my parents because they were very concerned about what they were going to do, how they were going to educate their children. So, my concern was mostly based on what they were feeling; how what were we going to do, you know, where were we going to school. How long it was going to last, you know.

Well my Uncle John and his wife had come down for a weekend, and I wasn't privileged to the conversation, and I don't know how the conversation went but our parents came out and told us we were going to New Jersey. He laughed; I was like going to New Jersey? (laughing again). And they say yea, your uncle going to take you up there and you going to school so that's what we did. They packed us up and I mean it was like a matter of a few hours to me;

it could have been longer than that, I don't know how long the conversation went. It was the same day they stopped by the house, I guess to say good-by and they got into this conversation about the schools, I imagine they had had this conversation before, and they put us in the car and took us to New Jersey. And that was like woo, that was the first year.

On the way to New Jersey, I remembered having thoughts, this anger about white people, you know, closing, messing up the family and now we got to go to New Jersey and I had no idea what sort of situation the school Mahwah Junior senior high school in Mahwah, New Jersey, and I had no idea about the balance of black kids and white kids so when my aunt took us to the school to enroll us, we find out that there is about 14 blacks and about 700 white kids, so here we go again, my mind is twisted up again. You know, I said wow, you know we just left a place that closed the school system down because they didn't want us to go to school with the white kids and now we are in a situation where we got all of these white kids and 14 black kids and they welcoming us with open arms. So, it was a culture shock. Yea, but everything went well.

Things didn't go that great in New Jersey as far as my aunt and her mother where we eventually stayed, because what happened was they brought us from Virginia and didn't tell this lady that they was going to, bring two kids with them. She already had two kids in the house. So, things were kind of rocky there, but we did make it through the year. So, we made it through the year and we came back to Virginia and I went to school in Stafford County about 35 miles from Washington, and my brother went to school in Amelia County.

I graduated in 62 at Stafford H.H. Poole, in Stafford, Virginia, and my brother graduated in 61 in Amelia, Virginia. My uncle came down for the summer and I asked him could I go back to New York with him and he said yea, so I am 18 years old and in New York and his father in law had a janitorial business that the father in law had given him part of it. At that time in New York, $10.00 would get you a job and they would send you on four, five, eight different jobs a day until you picked out the one you wanted. They sent me to a hospital, Jude's Memorial Hospital and I worked there and I went in as a porter, cleaning the floors and then there was an opportunity to be a transporter and I left there and transported patients from the rooms and then there was an opportunity to work in the dark room at this hospital in the ray department, so I got that and then they taught me how to take x-rays so, I was taking rays, but I didn't have a license, but at that time, they weren't stressing too much on that, so I was taking x-rays in the operating room at this hospital and I worked there for about seven years. Then somebody told me that they needed someone, a quality control person in this huge hospital at Columbia Presbyterian, so I went over there and they hired me. I wanted to come back to Virginia, I was married at that time, that was my first wife, so I came back to Virginia, I think it was '72, I brought the kids and her and everything. I worked at Stackpole in Farmville for I think it was a year. I said no, I can't do this, so I went back to New York, I did all of that in those hospitals, but I didn't have any training, so I had to go back to school and that was very difficult because I had these kids, but I did go back to school for Dental Ceramics. I made permanent bridges, jackets and crowns, and I did that for about 20 years.

If school had not closed, I don't know, my whole thing was I wanted to be a policeman, ever since I was a little kid, I wanted to be a policeman. The closest I got to it was working in corrections, but I really don't know because after I worked in the medical field as a dental ceramic I was real happy with that job, it was a lot of stress, but I don't know. I am just sorry that it happened and I just think how ignorant it was, it was a very ignorant move for the administration of Prince Edward County. I mean it's just hard to believe, even now, it's just hard to believe that this actually happened, you know so, every now and then I get these flashbacks of Farmville, the way it was before the Longwood took the neighborhoods and before the school closed and people had to move their families and break up their families. I think about that, you know, it really did a number on Farmville, it really did, so I still can't believe sometime that this actually happened (laughing). I ask myself how did this happen, how did they do this? And you got Cumberland County, Amelia, all these people and they kept the, you know the people probably had the same feeling, but they didn't close the school. So that's my thoughts. Now I am retired from corrections in Nottoway County in Virginia.

Anna Rosa Harrison

When school closed, I passed to the 10th grade. I found out about the school closing when my family called and explained. When school closed, I left for New York in July 1959 for the summer. I decided to stay and complete my education. I completed high school in 1962.

If I had known that people in the county were sending students to different areas, I probably would have come home. As an adult, I returned home, worked in Prince Edward County School System. I am retired.

Norman Carl Neverson

When school closed, I was in the 9th grade. I heard that school was closed in the county churches in June of 1959. When I heard that school was closed, my reaction was, I must leave Prince Edward County immediately. I worked in the pulp fields the months of June and July 1959 and on August 18th, I walked to Washington, D.C. and went to school. I was in the 9th grade that next year. I finished high school in Washington, D.C. Roosevelt High School on June 6, 1963. I graduated the year that schools reopened in Prince Edward County. I did not come back, but my brothers and sisters came back.

I am presently the CEO of an Instructional Management Company called Neverson and Associates.

The school closing of county Prince Edward County shocked many people, it hurt many people, but there were some who benefited from the school closing and I am one of those people. It gave me opportunities I would never have gotten in Farmville; a chance to enter college four years later and to go to George Washington University, Washington D.C. and to become a teacher, as many of my great leaders have been, and to see part of America I would have never seen before.

George T. Holcomb

When school closed, I had passed to the tenth grade. My parents and the community told me. My parents were farmers and sharecroppers.

When I heard school had closed, I didn't know what to think. I don't think it dawned on me what had happened. I kept hearing folks saying that they hoped schools would not be closed long.

I went for a little while to a one room building in Darlington Heights near where I lived. I then went to Charlotte County Schools using my brother's car to drive to the county line. I moved to DC in 1962 and went to night school for two years to get my GED. After becoming employed for the DC public Schools System, I went to school to get my engineer's license. When schools opened, I had already moved.

I am now a retired Chief Engineer after working 35 years in the DC Public Schools. I loved sports and athletics in school. I always wanted to work with children in a recreational capacity. I was always determined to make something out of my life regardless of the school closing. My parents stressed that you had to work hard to get what you wanted in life.

Etta Booker-Neil

When school closed, I was in the seventh grade. I found out about the schools, probably from the community and from my parents, that I can remember. When I found out that school was closed, I cried, I was disappointed, because I didn't think that schools were really going to stay closed, but I stayed out a year when we had to go back and forth to different churches to be taught so that we could stay refreshed and when that first year went by and that second year was coming up, that's when I realized this is for real, yes. I had an older sister who lived in Nottoway County, in Blackstone, Virginia. I stayed out one year and the next year, I went and stayed with her.

159

When schools reopened in Prince Edward County, which was in 64, I was in the 11th grade. I didn't attend any of them. I stayed in Nottoway County and graduated in 1965. I didn't come back.

I am a retiree now from government with the Department of Defense in Richmond in 2010. I stayed there with the government for 30 years. I'm volunteering and just enjoying my free time, but I also try to reach back out to Prince Edward County and help, because a lot was lost by some of the brothers and sisters in the county and they are still struggling with simple things like reading and I am trying to help out with that.

What would I have done if school had not closed? Woof, I had a lot of interest, but my childhood dream was to work with the airlines. I always wanted to be a stewardess (laughing). I love traveling even today and I always loved the airplane. So I figured well I'd be an airline stewardess and I'd just travel all over the world, but it didn't happen, yes.

I think the impact of the school closing impacted me now more than it did when it closed because even though I lost a year, I was still active because it was so many people that came out to our churches and kept training us, teaching us, but then when I went to Nottoway and finished my education and when I started working with the government I was able to do my four years of college through the government at Virginia State College in Petersburg, but I was blessed because my job instructed me to the site, we were at an army depot location in Richmond that brought the teachers to us. Once I got off my job, we had our classroom already set up and we took advantage of the courses there, so they provided for my four-year education in business.

But what hurt me more, what impacted me more when I came back home and started reuniting with Prince Edward County and just to see and hear the stories of what other people went through, you know, it still touches me real deeply and sometimes I hear their stories and I have to fight tears because I think while I was happy being in school, I had no idea what other people was going through.

So as much as I can I want to help people, even grown men and women, if I can help with their reading or fill out applications or apply for a job, which I do now for them at home. Some of them don't know computer skills, or whatever, but whatever I can help, I do that now, my own time, yes. I appreciate meeting the Prince Edward people now because I truly feel that I missed out on not knowing Prince Edward from the age of 12 or 13. I lost touch with everybody, now that we are 50, 60, 70 years old, it's like we reunited again. I lost a lot not knowing the neighboring people, you know? So, I do miss that, but I am trying my best to reunite, (laugh) yes.

Irene Watson-Hurt

When school closed, I was twelve years old in the 6th grade. I honestly don't remember how I found out that school had been closed. I wasn't happy because I couldn't get an education. I think I was out of school for a year and then they started this Free School at High Rock Church and I think I went there for about a year and then I went to Richmond and stayed with my great aunt for three years. Because my dad worked on the railroad, he was able to pay my tuition every semester so I could go to school to get an education. When Free school opened in Prince Edward, I came back to Prince Edward and stayed two years, I was in the eleventh grade. I finished the 11th grade and did not come back to the 12th grade.

Cynthia Johnson

 I had just completed the fourth grade when school closed. I found out about the school closing by my parents. When I found out that school was closed, my reaction was unbelievable. Because we were out for summer break, it was just any normal summer. That's what we normally do and when Labor Day ended, we couldn't go back to school. When school closed, I was here for one year, because everybody assumed that it was going to open back up. It was just a period of time it was going to open back up, but after being out of school for a year, my parents decided to move to Baltimore, then they packed up the whole family and moved everybody, my mother, my father, my three siblings and I went to Baltimore. Matter of fact, my father's brother and my cousins moved to Baltimore and they were living with us, so we all stayed in Baltimore and Baltimore became our lives. I went to school in Baltimore. When Free School reopened in 63, I was like in the eighth grade. I did not come back; I graduated there from Pauline Dunlap School in Baltimore. We had made a home there.

I am now retired and loving it. I retired with the Baltimore City Police and moved back to Prince Edward and worked for the school system for a few years and I retired as Assistant Principal at Prince Edward County High School. I have no idea what I would have done if school had not closed. I sometimes feel when school closed in Prince Edward was probably, I hate to say the word beneficial to me, but it was because I doubt very seriously if I had done the traveling that I have done or gone to the different places, the different types of jobs that I have done, had I been in Prince Edward my whole life, I had no idea what I would have done, because when I was here I had just turned 12 years old when we moved to Baltimore.

So at 11 years old, I had no idea what I wanted to do with my future. So I guess pretty much the only thing open was to become a school teacher and I hadn't really thought about that until I moved to Baltimore, once I moved to Baltimore, then I thought of becoming a teacher, but right out of high school I started working for the police and my idea always was, I knew I could work 30 years there and retire at 49, and my idea was always once I retired I would go back there and teach in the school system that refused to educate me. And that is what I did. I think it's a good idea for students now days to understand the importance of education because at a time in my life where education wasn't a choice, because it wasn't available. I think education is the best thing, especially for the young folks to do.

Sophia H. Jones

I was in the 5th grade when school closed. I found out about the school closing from our teacher, Mr. Power who told us. When I heard that school had closed, I was totally shocked. When school closed my mother had relocated to New Jersey, so we went to Patterson, New Jersey to go to school there. When school reopened here, since I had been in New Jersey for so long, I stayed there and continued in New Jersey. Principal Joe Clark, was my 7th grade-teacher.

My sister didn't want to go to the high school in New Jersey and she asked my mom could she come back home and go to school. My grandmother and grandfather were here, so my momma told her yes. So we went to elementary school and whites were there in the class she was familiar with. When she went to high school, she was in shock; she said it's too many white people. She told my mom. I wanted to go to Virginia, so my mom let her come back. I went to school in New Jersey because I was so use to them, it didn't bother me. I know I tried to be a cheerleader, or either a flag twirler, I didn't get it because they still had that race stuff about if you are not light enough you couldn't. So basically everybody who became a cheerleader was light. Nobody dark like me, after I graduate, they changed.

I finished school there and attended Junior State College and then being out of state, it was a lot of money for an out of state student, so I returned back to New Jersey and went to college there in Wayne, New Jersey, graduated, made …went back and got my first Master Degree and got a degree in certification in English as a second language. I love school, so I went back and got my second masters.

I taught elementary; I don't know how many years. I worked in Newark for one year, then I went to Patterson and worked at a day care center for one year, got into the public schools, taught there elementary, and then with ESL, I went on to high school and I retired three years ago, but I was going to try to make 40 years, but I only made 37 ½. I volunteer and I teach Bible study fellowship in White Cock in New Jersey and other things like volunteer at Gilbert's Club in New Jersey with patients that had cancer and at my church, I am involved in a lot of things with my sorority. I stay pretty busy and I enjoy it.

Education was important to my mom, out of all of her kids, I was the first to go to college. My sister went to college, she was a nurse for over 40 years now, so I was the teacher and she was the nurse and my mom said that was her two dreams, that she be a nurse or a teacher, so she said it is confirmed now. I am glad that I admired President Kennedy, because he was the one who made Free School possible, when I tell them about that they don't understand. I say people that been deprived of an education for five years, he opened up the schools.

I always wanted to become a teacher from a little girl, if school had stayed open, I would have loved to go to college, be a teacher, and I think my greatest joy would be here teaching in Virginia to give back.

Roy Pryor

When school closed, I was in the 5th or 6th grade. I found out about the school closing, well they were talking about it before school closed, you know you were hearing it from different people. We really didn't believe it though. When I heard about the school closing, in a way I was a little angry, just concerned you know, little angry in a way.

When school first closed, we went to Appomattox, we rented a house. We were living in this house, found out later on after we got in school and all, that part of the house was in Prince Edward County and part of it was in Appomattox. You could have walked across the road; you would be in Appomattox County and you could walk back across the road and you would be in Prince Edward County. So, when they found that out they came and got all 6 of us out of class and we had to leave Appomattox school. After they got all of us out of class, they told us why we had to leave, because the house was in Prince Edward, so after that we left there and we went to Baltimore.

When school reopened, I stayed in Baltimore, my sisters and brothers came back here, (in Prince Edward County) I finished in Baltimore. I came back home for maybe about a year or two years then I left and went to New York and then I came back home to stay in 1969.

I am retired now and still work part time for the county of Prince Edward. If school had not closed, I had a lot of things that I wanted to do. I wanted to go into business for myself, different things you know, I really hadn't decided, but I had a lot of things running through my mind of what I wanted to do. Well to me the way things are now and back then, it really didn't make any sense, you know because, I mean we were out of school, we were the only ones that suffered and actually it still happened the way they didn't want it to happen. You know they didn't want the black and white to go together, but they are still going together. And all that was unnecessary at the time I was going.

Joseph Randolph

 I was in the ninth grade when school closed. I went to Mary E. Branch School. I was in the 7th grade. Then I graduated to go to R.R. Moton to complete the 8th grade and I went to R. R. Moton High School for one year, and was passed to the 9th. I never made it to the ninth, that is when the school closed. I found out about the school closing through the system of the school. My reaction when I heard that school was closed – oh, I felt some kind of bad, because I could have graduated from there and probably be a lawyer or doctor, whatever to further my education.

After school closed well, I stayed out for about four months, then I went to Russell Grove High School in Amelia County, Virginia and I finished up down there. I stayed with my mom's friends, they kept me down there, they did an excellent job, they give me three meals a day, if I wanted clothes, they treated me real good and I appreciate the help. I had an automobile to drive back and forth and came home on weekends. When schools reopened in Prince

Edward County, I didn't come back.

If school had not closed – oh Lord knows, I could- no telling what I would have been doing. I just was sorry school closed, because no telling where people my age would have been, what they could have profited from, not being closed down and that threw me back quite a few years. Other than that, I made it. God always will make a way, no matter what happens.

Right now, I am retired from Tyson Food in Jetersville, Virginia in 2005 after 12 years. I worked at Stack Pole before I went to Tyson and worked up there for about five years. I have been with the fire department for 36 years, ever since they organized and I am the Chaplin at the Rice, Virginia firehouse. I am also trustee and treasurer at High Rock Baptist Church in Prince Edward County. I am doing just hobbies; honey do lists and taking care of my rental trailers.

Tawanna Jean Oliver

I was just promoted to the fourth grade when schools were closed. My third-grade teacher's name was Mrs. Ernestine Herndon. I found out about the school closings on the way from school. We were walking home and the high school kids were talking about the schools not going to be open the next year, that's how I heard about it. It was strange because we were getting out for the summer so a lot of time during the summer didn't think much about it, then when fall of the year came and it was time for us to go back to school, my mom and dad said there is not going to be any school, so my mother who had taught out in Hampden Sidney in a little one room school, taught us school by home school that first year.

On the second year that schools were closed, my father worked at Drakes Branch, Virginia, which is in Charlotte County, the county where he was born. He rented a house there and we moved, it was my mom, my dad, myself, my sister Sophia, my sister Barbara, my baby brother Freddie, my grandfather Percy Brown and my great grandfather George Price and they were retired and they were old.

When school reopened my parents came back to Farmville during the time of Free Schools. Because we owned our own home, it was just closed up, locked up and everything while we were away. We came to Farmville about once a week and we would always check on the house and we came by the house and sometimes just sit around, because furniture and things was still in the house, so we would just come by and check on the house, sit around, play in the yard.

I came back to school in Prince Edward; I went to Free School here and then I finished the ninth and tenth grade in Prince Edward, then I transferred to schools in Cumberland County Virginia.

I'm retired now as a Principal. I have 30 years in education. I have an under graduate and a graduate degree from Longwood College. I was an adjunct at Longwood because they needed someone in the home economics department. I have been a grants director for the Federal Government through title one student support services. They have programs that follow students from title one programs all the way through Upward Bound and student services and Rodney McNeal, so these are all government funded programs through five grants.

I wanted to be a designer and so I did not become a designer, I became an educator and I don't know what things would have been like. I know I would have gone to college anyway because my parents didn't have any other plans but except for us to go to college, so I don't know what would have been my story if school hadn't been closed. I have been in education for over 30 years. I talk to my students about the school closing, about the education, about its worth, about using their time wisely and about the people who came before them that gave their lives in some cases for them to have the freedom and the rights that they have, so that's been my quest for all of these years. They didn't like it when I said I was out of school for one year, my sister Sylvia was out two. When Barbara started school, I think that was the year we moved to Prince Edward. So she didn't miss any time from school. Freddie was too little, but I think the only thing I can say is that I feel that our young people today don't value an education as much as we did and I think it's because everything has come so easily to them.

Dorothy Paige Johnson

I was in the 9th grade when school closed. I found out about the school closing on the radio. It was very upsetting when school closed.

When school closed, I had an aunt who lived in Baltimore, so my mother packed me up and I went to Dunbar High School. They gave me a test and I passed it and remained in the same grade and graduated in the 12th grade.

When school reopened, I had graduated and went to New York, got a job and went to night school. I took some business classes to help me get a good job.

I have retired now.

I hated it when school closed, but I feel I learned more by leaving Prince Edward County. The black people really didn't have a chance to get a good job.

Florence Edwards

I believe I was in the 9th grade when school closed. I found out about it because I was probably being involved in it. I knew something was going on, probably through my parents and the older folks in the community discussing and I realized that I was not going to school. My reaction when I found out that school was closed, was quite umbilical as a young girl about 16 or 17 years old, and I didn't really know what was going, just something going on except that something was going on affecting the schools, so I kind of had to wait and see what was going on. I thought about it and in retrospect I think a little bit about it like Abraham in the Bible and not knowing where he was going, and I think that was certainly it was for me.

I think my parents made arrangements, I guess my mom, and dad was contacted by the Prince Edward County Christian Association and the group in Pennsylvania, the Quakers. They came and took a lot of students. They made arrangements for students to go away, with their parents' permission, to some of the schools. It was the decision, I guess offered to them by them or from different organizations, and so they took it for me. As far as I know no one else in my family went. I don't know why me.

When school reopened, I stayed on the course I was going, still not really knowing, pretty much having a good time, of growing and changing, and not afraid, naive in a lot of ways. I stayed as I said it was in the 9th grade and finished high school in Media or Ready, Pennsylvania.

I am retired in Farmville, not doing anything.

At times I would like to work, but it is difficult getting around. I don't really have a mindset for working hard, but I wouldn't mind after I get everything together, when that is, I don't know, do some volunteering. Give help to somebody. If school hadn't closed, I think, my initial plan was as a child playing on the lawn of our home, the small church that we attended, I really felt that the only calling for a Christian was to be a missionary.

So, I was inspired to do that and, in some sense, I did that, but I know that I didn't want to stop going, I didn't want to stop moving. I just moved with the flow, whatever happened, ok, let's do this. I think I like to add which is the essence of my life, and that is I like to think that wherever I had gone, whatever I'd done, that there was an element of strong faith and the Lord Jesus Christ, to guide and to mold my life because as I look back, I may not have been very conscious of that, I just wanted to be a good person. I think that as I look back it was truly him bringing me to a deeper faith. And I feel now that my faith is stronger than it has ever been and still growing and changing and that comes with a lot to trials and troubles.

Lucy Garrett

I was living with my grandmother. When she passed in 1959, I had to leave. I was in the 11th grade when school closed. I went to New York to live with my mother and sister. I went to a Girls High School, and that is where I met my husband later. He had gone to the Boys High School just a block away. I never came back to Prince Edward County. I got married and had children and moved to Mexico. I never knew anything that was going on in Prince Edward County until I went to college.

That summer I came back to Prince Edward County to visit and all the children was gone. When I asked my aunt about it, she told me that they went to school somewhere else and when I asked why, my aunt told me about the school closing. I went back to college and read up on it and researched it in my adult years and started reading up on things about Prince Edward County. Farming became difficult because kids had to go away to school. She remembered her cousin on a farm had begun to build him a house on his land beside his old house and had to stop building it and move to Cumberland, (the neighboring county) so his kids could go to school.

Tawana Sabbath

 When school closed, I was almost twelve years old and had completed sixth grade.

I don't remember hearing that the schools were closing until my parents started planning for my older brother and me to return to Baltimore for school. What I do remember is that things were in such a rush for us to get back to Baltimore.

I did not understand until years later the impact of the school closing. I knew that we were going to be in school regardless of the school closing. I must admit that I did not think about my classmates and what would happen to them. I may have assumed that everybody would find a school somewhere.

Our parents planned that my older brother and I would return to Baltimore with our father while my two younger siblings would stay with our mother in Prospect, Virginia at her father's home where we had lived for the school year.

Since we were temporarily living in Prospect due to our maternal grandmother's illness, we knew we would be going back to Baltimore at some point. That may also have kept me from focusing on the seriousness of the school closings in the area. I was moved to Baltimore County with my play cousin and her grandparents, while my brother lived with our father.

I was returning to familiar surroundings and old friends, so I was actually excited about my return. My brother was starting a new school in Baltimore City. I entered seventh grade while my brother entered eighth grade. My sister who had completed first grade in First Rock, Prince Edward County, attended school in our aunt's home where classes were held.

Our family moved forward educationally, with all four of us completing college. After graduating from Morgan State College, Ralph went on to law school and graduated from Boston University. I am also a Morgan alumna and hold the Master's and doctoral degrees in social work from Bryn Mawr College. Sylverna graduated from University of Maryland and then earned her Master's degree and Doctorate in the library science field at University of Pittsburgh. The youngest, Kelvin, graduated from Fisk University and entered the Air Force. Presently, my husband and I own a funeral home in Philadelphia, PA.

Until recently and only after touring the Robert Russa Moton Museum in 2013, I have not thought about the impact the school closings had on our peers. I had not even asked my cousins about their experiences. I did know that cousins in Cumberland County were taught by a teacher from Prince Edward County, Mrs. Hazel Carter. In reading about the experience of other families, I know that many of my peers did not complete junior high school, let alone high school. Since I was in sixth grade when the schools closed, that meant that many of my classmates would not have graduated. Interestingly we traveled to Prospect every summer after 1959 but I do not remember hearing anything about how my peers and cousins were faring. It is only now that I have even begun to consider what they experienced.

Wazir Yahya Shabazz

I think I was in the seventh grade when school closed. I found out about the school closing from community news. When I heard about it, the initial was shock, amazing fact that I wouldn't be going back to school.

After school closed, they told me about a program you could actually go, the church. First Baptist was actually sending kids out of the community in order to get an education. They were placed with families and I had relatives outside of the community. My first stop was Richmond. I lived with an aunt and uncle and I attended Walker High school and Armstrong High School, both in Richmond, Virginia.

When school reopened, I was maybe like 17 or 18. At that time I was getting my education in New York. I had two years in a community college.

Now, I work at the American Muslim Society, based in Chicago.

If school had not closed, I would have like to become an orator or writer. I believe the school closing was a negative experience, because it was when they use the term race, I don't believe that using the term, the true term Race, the word that normally precedes Race is human. The Race is one Human Race is unity. The word that they really wanted to use would be the word ethnic. Anytime you have individuality, you are talking ethnic. This comprised of the Human Race, as God said in his book, he created us in this manner in order for us to learn from each other, and truly this experience has taught us a very valuable lesson, that we are to learn from each other about our individuality as opposed to how Shaitan or divided. That cost animosity and hatred among the human family.

Edward Lockett

When school closed, I was in the 7th grade. I found out about the school closing by my parents. I had no real reaction. I never thought that schools would be closed that long. When I was not able to go to the 8th grade in the fall of 1959 is when it hit me that I had no place to go.

I attended a training school in Prospect, VA for two years before going to Appomattox County schools. Went to and graduated from Livingstone College in NC. I taught science in Prince Edward County High School for a year before being drafted in to the military. Spent three years in the U.S. Army.

My father worked for the Railroad and my mother was a stay at homemaker and worked as a cook in a restaurant after schools closed. When school re-opened, I stayed in Appomattox. I was in grade 10. I own my own my own business. I am also a minister.

Richard Miller

I was in the 8th grade when school closed. I found out that school closed when it didn't reopen the following year and people went elsewhere. I figured it out and people were talking what they were going to do and how they were going to make it. When I heard that school was closed, I felt terrible, I said it's going to be a whole bunch of people that's going to need some learning so I left here and went to New York and stayed a little while up there. I was in New York for 4 years and stayed with my sisters Carrie and Sadie.

When school reopened, I didn't come back. I was in Newark, New Jersey at that time. I stopped school and went to work, I had to do something for myself until I was 62 and I retired to give the younger one's time to go in there and do something. If school had not closed, I would like to have been a truck driver; I drove for a while, freight and drove taxi. I had a hack license I would have to put in the taxi. I really wanted to get a job where you could work 20 years and retire.

School closing was a terrible thing, by you being black you not going too far in this town, they had a school built specially for them and they made us look bad. They figured we can't do it, and if you could do it, they would hold you back.

Frances Johnson-Hicks

I was in the 6th grade when school closed. My parents told us that the school would be closing. When school had closed, I couldn't understand why. When school closed, my father packed all his stuff up in a car and put whatever he could put in the trunk of a car and took us to Baltimore. Actually, we lost a year because we thought that school would be reopen, we couldn't imagine that school would not re-open, so after about six month or so, when they talked like schools may not open again, my father just packed up and moved to Baltimore. I went to school in Baltimore, actually we just made Baltimore our home. When school re-opened, I stayed in Baltimore. Actually, I think by school closing, it actually gave my whole family an appreciation for education. Out of the four of us, we all went to school and 3 out of four went to college.

Now, I am happily retired from the Baltimore Police department and I moved up the ranks to Sergeant. I retired as a sergeant. During that time, I also worked for the Mayor of Baltimore City and worked for Curt Smoke, the first black elected mayor of Baltimore City. If school had not closed, actually, now I can look back and think about the school closing, it may have been a blessing in disguise because had I stayed here, I don't know what I would have actually done. I don't know that I would have stayed here and gotten a Master Degree for college. I took associate Arts, a Bachelor and then I finished with a Master Degree.

At the time I left, I guess for a long time I was, after I got older and realized what was going on, I guess I had quite a bit of anger about the whole situation and about Caucasian people, the white group, but I got to the point where now I realize that they were in a lot of ways as caught up as well as we were. You know some of the poor whites you know, and I am just thankful for where I am, I really am. You know that I can look back now and not be angry. I am beyond that and be able to just go on with my life and be thankful I had the parents that I had with the foresight to take us, I guess to pack up and leave to some place you never been and make a life for us. At first, I thought I would never come back. I swore I would never come back on my whole family and then when I came about 12 years ago, nobody could believe it, my family came to the wedding because they couldn't believe that I had moved back to Virginia. But now I am good, I am good.

Wyatt Vaughan

 I was in the sixth grade when school closed. I think it was about somewhere the mist of the summer when I found out really that it had closed. This was this lady that my mother worked for. My mother went up there washing some clothes for her and took the clothes back, and she kinda blurted it out. She said something like yea. We are going to fight it until the end and momma came back and took that door and let us know that school was closed.

I think it was about a year, that first year, it didn't really dawn that it was taking place. I think by seeing the white children on the bus, so when school closed it didn't dawn on me until that second year the school closed, when we use to go up there to have classes and you kinda knew that school was closed. That was right along the 60's. We stayed at home. My daddy was still working up north because to make extra money, so he could send money home to mama. I have 3 brothers and 3 sisters. All of them stayed home, but my older graduated in 52. I came back, but it didn't work out so I left trying to pay for the cars and bills I made. Fact of the matter the first job I had was carpenter work.

I became pastor of the Antioch church in Blackstone. Right now, I am a full-time pastor, then you look back education, social, all of this played a role in this. He has taken me on one awesome journey. A professor from Washington University came down to interview me and my brother. We played at the Smithsonian Institute and Gospel Travelers is NOW in the Smithsonian Institute. They have begun coming from Detroit Michigan from Monaco records and they want us to perform here. God has been good.

Phillip Walker

I was in the ninth grade and passed to the tenth grade when schools closed. I found out about school closing through the media, people and talking in general, actually it was out there everybody knew that it was closing down at the end of the school year. My parents did not talk about it. When school closed, I said, well I am going to have to do something. I moved to Connecticut and I worked two years and I saved my money up and came back and enrolled in Appomattox, because my cousin was teaching there and she got me in school, and that's how I continued my education for three years. I graduated in 1964 at Carver Price in Appomattox. When free school opened in '64 I was already a senior. I already had everything together so it didn't make sense in me coming back. I already had three years in the books in the Appomattox, so I was ready to come out. My parents supported me, but I had to make a choice, either go to work or either try to get enrolled in school somewhere.

I went to Connecticut to go to work. I was 16 at the time. Actually, you couldn't get a job unless you had working papers. If you didn't have a social security card, you could not work in Connecticut until you were 18. That man told me, in order to get a half way decent job, you got to have at least a high school education. So I said, I reckon that I better finish school and I came back home. I went to school and graduated. I enjoyed it, because after I saw I couldn't make it without it, I finished school.

It was an experience. A lot of people that did not go back to school when school closed, I think they regret it because you really need it. The reason I got it was that man told me in order to get a decent job, you have to at least get a high school education. So, I made it, and here I am. I am now retired and a professional landscaper.

Walter M. Brown

I was in the third grade when school closed. I found out about the school closing because I was in it. When I heard that school had closed, I really didn't want to believe it. When school closed, being that my grandfather lived in Cumberland County, Virginia, right across the bridge from Farmville, I went to Cumberland County. When school reopened, well, I came back for the Free Schools. I stayed there for a while until I ended up in New Jersey and after I ended up in New Jersey, I actually didn't graduate from Prince Edward, but I got my GED through the Army.

Now I work for Hampden Sydney College, getting ready to retire, been up there for 21 years. If school had not closed, well I would like to have been a good Samaritan. Help people do things. I always try to be the best you can. Well, I think to myself, it was a very hard thing to swallow, I wouldn't like for anybody else to go through it.

Darlene Walker -Brown

I was in the 8th grade when school closed. I do not remember how I found out about school being closed. I was very sad when we heard that schools were closed. I lived in Prince Edward County, the town of Farmville, for one year, I was so happy because I got to ride the bus one year from Mary E. Branch School, (currently the Moton Museum) to the high school. Then I had to move back to my home place in Cumberland (the neighboring county) and live with my mother and father who moved too. I was very upset when I had to leave Farmville and go to live in Cumberland

County again; I felt very sad.

I stayed in Cumberland, but was still going to Prince Edward County Public Schools, because for a distance over Cumberland Bridge, it was still considered Prince Edward. I remembered how frightened I was having to cross the bridge each day, twice a day that had planks of wood that had pieces missing and you could see the water below if you looked down. I had to look before crossing to see if any cars were coming, because if you were on the planks at the same time it shook the wooden planks and that was very frightening.

I went to Luther P. Jackson High School in Cumberland County and graduated. I finished high school in Cumberland in 1963, the year free school opened in Prince Edward County. I did not lose any time from school. The only thing I can say is that Luther P. Jackson did not have a Gym, did not have a cafeteria that was the biggest disappointment in going from R.R. Moton.

Lucille Baker Boyd

I was coming out of the 7th grade going into the eighth grade. I found out about the school closing, well, I was young back then, so we only had stuff like that on the news. It's not like now, the news was late evening and they said that we wouldn't have any schools. I made it until June, and they said it wouldn't open in September. I felt kind of scared and it was hard for me because you never did anything but, you automatically went to school.

I had an aunt to come and pick me up that lived in Baltimore and registered me in school in Baltimore. I finished school there in Dunbar High School. I went to Dayton, Ohio the first year and the second year I was at Norfolk School. I am retired from Proctor Gambling.

Joseph Hicks

I was in the 10th grade when school closed. I heard that school was closed from my parents. I probably was too young to realize what was going on. When school closed, my father was a carpenter and I went to work with him. When school opened, by that time I was married and had a family, I did not go back to school. I probably was too young at the time to realize what was going on, what the outcome of it when school closed to know how I felt when I heard it. I am retired now from construction. If school had not closed, I would have liked to go into the Air Force and fly a jet airplane. I would have liked to have been an airplane pilot. After I had a family and I got into construction. I did go back to school to get my GED in the early 90's.

I think the Board of Supervisors should have been sued a big sum of money for not funding the school system and closing the schools down.

Lawrence (Lloyd) Wise, Jr

When the schools closed, I was going into the 11th grade. I heard about it from the teachers and I was shocked. I felt real bad about it. When school reopened I hadn't done much of anything but work at the hospital and Bob's Supermarket. I had so many jobs, you know.

I didn't go back to school. I think if school had not closed, I could have bettered myself, you know. I wanted to learn a little bit more and thangs like that, because maybe I could of taught someone else. The closing of the schools I was disappointing, very disappointed, very difficult and very hurtful.

Robert Baldwin (Mann)

 I was in the second grade when school closed. I found out about school closing because well, we went on our summer break and didn't go back to school and my mother told me that school was closed. When I heard that the schools were closed, I was scared because it was a lot of things that went with it. They were saying things like, don't be caught by yourself away from home, all these types of things were going on and they were saying that people might try to do something to you, if you were by yourself. We were scared to go to Cole's store and Ms. McKnight store (which was about 3 minutes from where I lived) places like that where we had normally been walking. You know, we lived right behind the schools and the stores were on Main Street. That's where we use to travel with our soda bottles and go to get cookies and stuff. My mother told me you know, we couldn't go to the store, because my mother was a little involved in the civil rights movement. So, I was real scared, and we had to stay at a certain area around our house, close to stuff in our neighborhood and couldn't go to stores and stuff. We couldn't go where the schools were and that kind of hurt because we used to go to Mr. Coles or Mrs. McKnight's store where a lady named Sue Belle was working.

When school closed, I think I missed almost a year of school and then my mother moved us to Baltimore, Maryland. I started school up there in the third grade and finish my schooling up there, I graduated in Baltimore. We didn't come back when school reopened. When I came back, I was grown, I was 24 or 25 years old, but we kept up with the progress of school; we realized when it was open and everything because it was in all the Jet magazine, which kept the story going in those Jet magazines. Matter of fact I still got some of those jets.

I came back to Farmville, Virginia in 1978 and I went to work at State Farm Correction System and retired in 2007. If school had not closed, well I would have like to have finished school here where I was born and raised. I had to leave and was raised somewhere else. I would like to have stayed; I never liked the city; lived there all that time and I never liked it. And when I came back here to visit, I made up my mind then that I would eventually move back and that's what I did. I moved back here. I love it here; I still love Farmville. If I won a million dollars I would live right here.

Well I don't want to add a lot to my story, I don't have any – you know at one time I had a lot of animosity to people that caused things to happen like that, and of course I didn't know exactly who to blame, but for a long time I couldn't forgive, let it go, but now I let it go and give it to God. I am willing to forgive and let it go but I never will forget because there are scars that leave you thinking about it often. I think back to it, matter of fact my whole life has been based on those incidents with the school. Every time I think about it, in Farmville, every time I make a decision, I think about back then and how it was.

Well, I actually get sad when I think about my mother, because my mother, during the time, the first year when they closed the schools, my mother got involved in all the demonstrations and the civil rights movement and stuff and I remember her telling me about downtown at the college shop, and they would try to get their rights and go in and sit down and eat and stuff like that. It was a peaceful and nonviolent demonstration. So, you know, those scars are still in me. You know, I never will forget that stuff, you know because that was my mother. So, you know it's a lot of scars, but I am willing to, you know, let it go. I forgive them. I have since gotten it all out of me so it doesn't bother me as bad. I will NEVER forget it and I am going to see that my kids know the history of it, because a lot of kids really don't know. And too, they owe people, people that withstood all of this stuff, they owe them because it wouldn't be possible for them to be where they are so they actually owe them and should be proud. They actually should be proud for the people who fought for them, even the ones, especially the ones who didn't go to school because of it, we really owe them.

So, I forgive them, but like I said my mama was involved in a lot of that stuff and when we moved to Baltimore, she kept up with it. She would buy the Jets and newspapers and whatever. Like I say, I got some jets now that belong to my mother with the Prince Edward story in it. "Yea, you are welcome to borrow them." Believe it or not your brother was involved in it, Earl was maybe a couple years older than me and one thing Earl used to do when we were kids, the comic books, he would have comic books and them comic books kept me learning, taught me how to read.

When the originals Spiderman, Fantastic Four, Kid Cote, all of that stuff, Earl had all of those books and he would let me read them too. And if I got any I let him read them. That's how I learned to read. I was in the second grade so I actually hadn't gotten that far in reading, but I kept reading the books, I kept reading the comic books and I learned how to read reading comic books. When I got to Baltimore, they put me in my regular grade because I already knew how to read. But if it hadn't been for those comic books, I don't think I would have learned how to read. And I was a comic book fanatic and Earl was too. That's why I say he helped me a whole lot, because I learned a lot from him too. If it hadn't been for him, and those comic books, who knows?

Elsie Ferguson- Cham

I was in the eighth grade when school closed. I found out about the school closing through Reverend Griffin and Martin Luther King. When I heard that school would close, I felt bad because we didn't have enough education to finish school. I had to come to New Jersey to finish school. After I graduated from Central High School, I went to the nursing school of college engineering and I went to school for a licensed practical nurse and worked in the city hospital they have here for 14 years. When school opened, I was still in Newark, New Jersey, I didn't come back.

Now sometimes I do secretary work, I do volunteer work, sing and do missionary work. I am on disability now; I don't work anymore because of my health. If school had not closed, I would have liked to have finished school. I felt bad about the school closing and the integration and the segregation because we didn't have any rights in a lot of things and we didn't have rights to do this and rights to do that and it was bad, and the whites didn't like you and they took the black people through a lot of changes.

Leslie Lycurgus Hall, Jr.

I was in the 6th grade when school closed. I found out about
the school closing in Prince Edward County during the
summer of 1959. I asked my father what that was all about
and he finally told me. My father was the Principal at Mary
E. Branch at the time. When I heard that school was closed,
I was happy because I thought I wasn't going to have to go
to school. I think it was August when he told us we were
going to Cumberland. I was not a happy camper, no. It
changed back to reality when my father told me we were
going to Cumberland, (the adjoining county), to go to
school. During the latter part of that summer I went with
daddy on several job interviews; thank goodness, he didn't
take any of those. Schools reopened in Prince Edward
County when I was a senior, it would have been a bit of a
waste of time to come back. I graduated from Luther P.
Jackson High School in Cumberland County.

Now I am retired from the main Richmond Post Office on
Brook Road. When they closed our schools, they gave me a
disconcert for whites that I don't think I would have had
otherwise. I watched them smile in my daddy's face while
they shut the doors to the school. I watched them trying to
shine him along like he was stupid. I spent quite a bit of
time with daddy. I was with him during the summer when
he was working because I was at the little playground until
12:00 and until 2:45, I was inside with him. So, I saw a lot
of the comings and goings. I have mistrust in trusting
whites, even now, more so now.

Naja Griffin- Johnson

I was in the third grade when school closed. My father and
mother told us in a family meeting which they said was
very important. I was confused, sad, because it was the

center of my being. We went to stay with our grandmother for the first year in New Jersey (my mom and the kids). My dad stayed in Farmville. We came back and my mother homeschooled until the free schools opened.

 I attended the free schools for one year, then a year at Robert R. Moton High before going to Palo, CA for my last three years of high school. When schools re-opened (Prince Edward Public Schools). I would have been in the 8th grade, but I'm not sure why (after testing) I was put in the 9th grade. I am currently living in California–retired–enjoying my grands and splitting my time between California and Virginia to help care for my mother.

If school had not closed, I would have most likely stayed in Farmville; graduated from Moton; married the guy I was in love with (name withheld intentionally!). Definitely would not have ended up in California. Would have finished college in four years and not have spread out furthering my education over years! I worked in advertising and at BET for some time in Production Coordinating.

The school closing changed the lives of many including mine. It changed my childhood and made it necessary for my parents to make decisions to send us to different cities/states. So, we missed enjoying the life we had known all of our lives in a place we loved. There can never be an explanation that can make any sense as to how this happened in America!

Many Male students chose a career in the military. Here is a story on how they maneuvered through this journey.

Samuel Baldwin

 I was in the first grade when school closed. I don't remember how I found out that school closed. When I did realize that school had been closed-- how I felt? I felt that the white man had done us wrong. They have done me wrong all my life. I was one of the people who benefited from the schools in the churches and schools at Mrs. McKnight store and school down at Mr. Miller's Dentist Office. Yea, Mr. Miller had the books in the basement, hundreds and hundreds of books. Yea, he used to give me a book every time I went there, he would give me a book. I couldn't read, couldn't write, but I would have a book.

When school closed, I was here for about two years and then I went to Baltimore. First, I went to Baltimore to stay with relatives and then I eventually went to different schools in and outside of Baltimore. At that time, I never did learn to read really good, and soon as I could quit school, I quit. I did not come back here to Prince Edward County when schools reopened. I came to visit in the summer time when school was closed for the summer, I came here to visit and stay with my Aunt Margaret.

I am retired from Walmart, but I was disabled through VA, so I don't work anymore. I always wanted to be a barber. I am a barber.

If school had not closed, I think I would have gotten an education. I think I would have been a more productive person and I think I would be good at it, business and making money, and I wasted so many years, so many years of doing the things I wasn't supposed to do and I can't get it back.

I went into the military at the age of 17 and went into the army. I stayed in there two years, went overseas and stayed over there for a while. I still always visited Farmville, always, always, you know. Most of the people I visited are dead and gone, why so many had to go away from here, so many, on both sides, family and friends. I pray for them, I pray for my enemies, you know.

Linwood Harris

 I was in the 9th grade passing to the tenth-grade. I would have been in the 10th grade come September when school shut down. I found out about the school closing from my parents. They were discussing it. There was five of us in school at that time and they shared that information with us. That they had to make a decision on what to do with five children. I am not really sure how I felt, how my reaction was, but I remember discussing it with my mom about where I would go to school. At that particular time, she wasn't sure but come August, she made up her mind to send me to Jersey, and that wasn't a good reaction, because I didn't really want to go to New Jersey (laughing).

The summer we stayed here in Farmville, but come August, I was sent to Pleasantville, New Jersey which is right off of 96 to live with my sister and brother who were there, to go to school up there. I really had a negative attitude about going to school in the city, because I wasn't a city person and uh, that didn't go over very well, the first year I was there and it didn't improve and I was hoping I could come back home, but nothing was going on here in Farmville to get me back home. Then I started encouraging my mom to let me go into the military. I was 17 then. I started to encourage my mom, which she really didn't like, but after working on her, my father was yea, yea, let's do that, but my mom said no, no, no, but after I changed her mind, talking with her pleading with her, begging with her whatever it took and she finally gave in and I went into the military and which was a true blessing.

I look at it today, as it was a blessing from God to shut the school system down to allow me to get away, because I wasn't always, in Prince Edward County at that time. I wasn't where I should have been as a 10th grader, so going into the military, things totally changed my life. It changed my outlook on life and immediately gave me a career. I got in just under the radar. So when I got to my first duty station with some friends, my training officer told us, there was five of us, that we was not going to stay in because we were not high school grads, but he offered us a unique opportunity. He told us if we were willing to work at night, he would allow us to go to the American High School in Troy Fontran France, which took in all the dependent children in that particular region and which was a golden opportunity. We all five agreed, so we went to regular school during the day like we would do in Prince Edward. We graduated with our diplomas after a year and a half. We all graduated and we were blessed. I stayed in the military for 27 years. (laughing) and so my diploma is like most kids, it would say, I went to this high school dah de dah, I did too, but mine say Troy Fontrane France.

Now I am retired twice, from the military and from a firm called Carbone of America which makes car parts, automotive brushes designed to make electricity and allow the vehicle to start or wipers to go and stuff like that. I did that for 16 years, so I retired from there also. But because I like to keep busy, after retirement for four or five months, I got bored and now I drive the school buses for Prince Edward County schools, the same one that closed. Now for about eight years. I think school closing was a blessing for me. Going back over my life, at 16 years old, I don't want to say I wasn't' pushed in the right direction, I just wasn't fired up about it.

If I was to go back and summarize the whole thing, I look at my whole life and I am thankful that I was able to leave Farmville, leave Prince Edward. And when I thought of coming back, my reason for coming back was because I had parents here, but I didn't come back here to get an education, but I believe I am back here because there is a need for someone to speak out and talk to young children and encourage them. When I was very young, I always watched police officers and always thought it would be nice to be a police officer. I think it kind of lead into what I been talking about, helping people. I have been talking about helping people all my life and I with my military career I was about helping people, but I always had this desire to be a state police officer.

The military never crossed my mind until I was in a situation where I didn't like being in. I saw commercials and ads about military people and it's kind of made me open my eyes and I said you know what? The military can do this for me what I can't do for myself. And it was my way out of getting out of New Jersey, that I didn't like, so I used the military to get out of New Jersey, but in the beginning I really wasn't planning on staying for no 27 years (laughing) because after I got so many years in, I still put in an application for a State Police. Yea, I did, I put in for Virginia, Maryland and New Jersey and I was getting close to the end of my contract in the military so I put the application in. Nobody answered my application, so I had to make a choice, either get out with nothing or stay in so I decided to stay in rather than to lose all of my time and my rank. Shortly after I re-enlisted for 6 years, I got a letter from the Virginia State Police, (laughing) oh my gracious, but it was too late then. So, I went ahead and stayed in the military, which was probably a blessing, because I was doing pretty much the same thing in the military that I would have done as police officer. My military career was in military intelligence.

Wilbur Dillard

I was 4 years old when school closed. I do remember as a small child, I went to Branch I and Branch II in Prince Edward County. My older brother (deceased) was affected by the closing of schools in Prince Edward; he was 2, but me and my brother was not old enough to go to school. When it was time for us to go to school my mother took us over to my great grandmother's house in Buckingham, and we had to go to a one room school house called Oak Grove and Galway. My grandmother took on two teachers, Mrs. Valarie Wilson and Mrs. Sheilds and they taught us, and Mrs. Josephine Bland who preached at Oak Grove. I actually think I was something like 4th or 5th grade when we moved to Baltimore, Maryland.

I found out school was closed because I was wondering why I had to go to school in Buckingham and my mother told us that because the school was closed in Prince Edward County. Once they reopened school my mother moved us to the Prince Edward County School System.

If school had not closed, I would (pause) kids back then had an imagination that ran wild. I never thought about being a doctor or nothing like that, but I had thought about being a lawyer or a prosecutor.

Being young, you never really knew what was going on as far as race and stuff like that because back then you were raised in a Christian family way and you weren't exposed to a lot like when we moved to Baltimore. The things I experience as a young man during that time, I was exposed to everything and one thing that sticks in my mind, I didn't realize it until I actually saw it with my own eyes. It was when my father and grandfather and two brothers went fishing at the Appomattox River on 15 in Prince Edward. When we came out there was a little restaurant on top of the hill on right hand side. I think it was called Dave Amos or something like that. My father was home from the service and he wanted to take us on the hill to get us some ice cream cones. So, we walked up on the hill and when he walked in the door, he stood there for such a long time waiting. He asked the waitress can I be helped, and she came to him and she said I'm sorry, we don't serve N in here. I think that was the first time I ever heard the word N.

My grandfather told my father, Coley, come on let's go and he said no, I am not going anywhere, I've served my country, I did my duty for my country and all I want to do is just get my boys an ice cream cone. The owner came out and told my father, you are not getting anything here, you need to get your N so and so out of here, so my grandfather was saying, please come on, please come on, and my father said I'm not going nowhere until I get served. My daddy got in a fight with the owner. And the next thing I know they called the county cop named Jack Campbell. He came in and daddy got in a fight with him and he kind of blindsided him with a billy stick and they hauled them off to jail.

That was the first time I really felt what was going on, because I just thought that people were people. But as I looked back on it, the way people were treated at that time, because we were small kids. We use to walk to the store and we wanted to walk along the road. My grandmother told us, no we can't do that. We had to walk in a path in the woods. They used to have a path to walk along about 10, 15, maybe twenty feet off the highway and you had to do that so nobody would try to run over you or throw bottles at you.

As started getting older, I just looked, I kind of wondered why people still say, why do you still feel that way. Well, if you go back and you look and you see exactly how blacks were treated back then, just like they was dirt, and looked at what they went through, and what they had to do. I can imagine people, the first people that say, that's it. No more and I can imagine why they said it. No more, they got tired of all the hangings, the burnings, no jobs and the disrespect, they got tired. They got fed up, they said no more, we want our rights.

I just hope that someday, the younger generation that's out there now, can stop killing each other and stop doing these things to each other and try to help each other, and better themselves. All they have to do is just go back and look and see what Black folks went through. That's a hurtful thing to think that people went through all that disgrace, humility.

I did ten years in the military, the United States Army. Getting back to how blacks were treated, when I finished my training at Fort Knox Kentucky, I was going to take my MOS training, is what your job is going to be while you are in the military. We were leaving Fort Knox, Kentucky going to Fort Jackson, South Carolina and we had to go through Memphis, Tennessee. The bus stopped at the bus station and we went in and this was in the early 70's, and we went in to be served. It took so long time. The governor of Kentucky, his son, joined the service and it just so happened, he was in our company and we were going to Fort Jackson together and we were standing there waiting to be served at the lunch counter of Memphis, Tennessee, He told us, yaw come on let's go, and we said why man we want something to eat, and he said man, they are not going to serve us here. They're just gonna make us wait, wait, wait. So let's go, and we walked out.

I had stopped at another little store and bought me a candy bar, and was walking down the street. When I finished with the candy bar, I see this trash can, which I thought was a trash can, and I raised the top on it to throw the wrap in it. This guy stopped me and he said man, don't do that, and I said why, ain't nothing but a trash can. He said no, it's' not. He said look above it and it had a little asterisk marker sign on it. It was a laughing barrel. They were put on the street for Black people. A black person could not laugh openly on the street; if he wanted to laugh, he had to put his head in that barrel. They still got them on the streets right in Mississippi. They got a little gold, black steel sign, called the Laughing Barrel. I could not believe that.

Then once I got out of the army, I went back to Baltimore working for the American Racing commission working with thoroughbred horses. I moved back to Prince Edward and got a job in Nottoway Correction Center; I worked there until I retired. I have been retired for 14 years.

At the end of the five-year journey, there were numerous families of children who had missed schooling for the entire five years. They will tell how this affected them and their siblings.

John Wallace Hurt

When school closed, I was in the first grade and passed to  the second grade. It was 12 of us, 6 girls and 6 boys. My brother who was two years older than I was, he went to the high school. I had one sister who had graduated. I found out about the school closing from my mama. I was excited to go to school and it wasn't anything to do but go to school. That was the only thrill we had, to go to school.

When school reopened, we had been out of school so long. When we did go back to school, now that I think about it, it must have been for the teachers, you know, trying to teach a great big grown kid, and like I said during that time, that was in town and things like that, they had gone to school. They weren't quite as uninformed as we were. But instead of grading us for our ability, they just grade us by our age. That made it very uncomfortable, you know you go to school and sit in school, they had all the answers from Ms. Coley's class. I think her class was third grade and I could remember her and another teacher named Ms. Belemy had words about it. I remember Ms. Belamy saying you can't expect them to do like other kids, but at that time they didn't think, but they would try to push you through according to your age. They couldn't have a 13 year old sitting with a 6 year old, so you got frustrated like that and you couldn't do that. I think this was around third or fourth grade, I know I went from Mary E. Branch I, when it closed and when it opened up. I went to Mary E. Branch II and then from there, I went to Worsham and that was even worse, because that was a higher grade, and we just couldn't do it; frustration and stuff back then. I reckon during that time, being a single mom, it just wore her out trying to get us to go to school, so we just wouldn't go back. So I am saying if school was like it is today, if kids was been tested when they went back for their ability to know what to do, it would have been a lot different.

Right now, I am in school called Ellis Acres Buckingham County and each week, it seems like it's harder and harder. It's more challenging and its more rewarding, now because I don't have to compete with nobody, not on my ability. It's great because I learn a whole lot, you know I still have a problem with the phonics, you know, I don't know about everyone else, but phonics is everything. If you don't have phonics, you can't sound the words out and stuff like that, with proper instruction they can teach you, can come to a word that you don't know. They encourage you to keep reading and you come back and you find out what that word is. I am in class with some who have a 11th and 12th grade education and can't write in cursive, but they all graduated. They went through the school system, sort of like me. There are several times I could have had my GED or diploma or whatever, you know, I probably couldn't have read, matter of fact one of the people asked me when do I think I will be ready for my GED test? I told him anytime you all think so, but GED is not what I am looking for. I am doing this to better myself, have more confidence in myself that really is what it was all about. I went back to school, not the preaching part, but the religion part, reading the Bible and stuff like that.

I am still working, going to school two times a week, sub pastoring a church, doing one on one tutoring on Fridays. I had to drop the other lady that was tutoring me because once my job at Buffalo Shook closed, I couldn't afford to pay her, but I miss her real bad, because she was the only one teaching me phonics. If school had not closed what I would have like to have done – that's no telling, that is another thing, in our generation, we really lost. I would have loved to have been a professional baseball player. I still love baseball; I look at it on television every chance I get. And coming up, there was a lot of baseball players in us, but we didn't have the schooling, we weren't connected to get into college; at that time, you had to go to college. It's not like it is now, because you had to go to college to play pro ball. Now if it had been like it is now, you know, they are drafting right out of high school.

The same question was asked of me when we went to Richmond by the Governor then. He asked me what would I like to do? I told him and it's still my feeling right now. I would like to have a shot of at least five years of being in school every day; no work, no work related, no bills. I would like to go to school five years like an ordinary student, and I really think with my mind set like this, I really think I could accomplish what I need to do, five or seven years because, now I know what it is, not to be playing around with, what to be doing.

That would be what I would like to see, even at my age, two years before retirement. I would like to be able to right now to retire full retirement and be in a place Even Ellis Acres. I can't do it because two of the classes is at night and two during the day. I don't call myself smart, but I am a long way from being dumb. My reason, I would love to do it for the ministry, the other reason, I am not doing it for money, title or what, it would just say that I did it, I got it, and look back to say that you know, you slowed me down, you gave me a detour, but you didn't stop me. I work for the state, but without an education or computer skills, you can forget about the jobs like a supervisor, a superintendent, you will never get a job like that. I have had co-workers and bosses ask me, how come you aren't no superintendent.

Thomas Hughes

I was in the ninth grade when school closed. I found out from the media that school had been closed. I felt down hearted when − (a pause), I think they deprived me of my education. I didn't go away when school closed, I stayed here and I worked. When school opened, I went back to school and stayed there until I finished. I graduated from Robert R. Moton High School.

Right now, I am retired from painting at Ayers Building Supply. If school had not closed - I like what I am doing now, painting. If school had not closed, maybe I would have been in better shape or had a different outlook − if school hadn't closed, maybe I would have done things different.

Mattie Carey Barksdale

I was about 12 years old, 6th grade when school closed. I found out about the school closing by people talking and my sisters, because they were in higher grade than I was, they knew it before I did. While school was closed, I was the youngest and I didn't get to go away to school because I was too young. I mostly stayed at home, I read a lot of books. Then some teachers came from New York down to some kind of center on Griffin Blvd, (was Ely Street) and they taught us classes down there and the teacher that I had, I forgot the name, they took two of us out of our class back to New York with them for the weekend and while we was over there, they took us places, bought us clothes, yea and everything and we had a nice time. And then at our church, we had an old schoolhouse up at New Witt Church and some of the parents would get together and teach us there. We used to go up there every Saturday. The old-school house is not there anymore, we joined it to our church now. When the school reopened, I went back to school. I was in the eighth grade because we had to take tests to see what grade to put us. I stayed the whole time and graduated from R.R. Moton High School.

If school had not closed, I think I would have furthered my education but then you know, I always wanted to be a mother and wife. That was my whole thing, but then it closed I still was a wife and mother, but I did little odd jobs when my husband, (Thomas Barksdale) was in the army. I cleaned house, I loved children, I use to babysit a lot, that was my main thing. About the school closing, I hated every bit of it because I didn't think it was fair for any of us and we lost out on a lot

Now I am retired. I use to work at the Winn Dixie Grocery Store, until I had my first child, that is, when I stopped work, and when she got in school, I did little odd jobs, but when he retired, I say I was coming home and retire too, that's what I did so we could travel.

Victoria (Anna Belle) Booker

 When school closed, I was 9 years old in the 4th grade at Mary E. Branch Elementary School. Mrs. Ernestine Herndon was my teacher. I found out about the school closing when we went to school and we had our books to go in. The principal was standing in the door and told us, I am sorry you don't have no school, they closed the school down. I remember that, those big chains on the door. When I found out that school

was closed, I cried, we don't have school. What are we going to do? Wasn't anything for us to do. White folks closed it up. White folks had schools, but black folks didn't have no school and we couldn't go to the white folk's school.

While schools were closed, I didn't go anywhere. We were too young to go anywhere. I stayed here in Prince Edward County until school opened. When school opened, I was in the ninth grade. I went to R. R. Moton High School and finished the 10th grade. I left and went to the Community College. After that I went to the Skill Center in Crewe, Virginia and got a certificate in nursing. I also took up seamstress while I was in Crewe. I stayed with a lady and came home on the weekends. I left Virginia and moved to Patterson, New Jersey and went to Eastside High School and received another nursing certificate and worked at Saint Joseph Hospital in New Jersey. I also worked at this place, Diet factory in New York City until it was transferred to New Jersey.

Now I am retired due to illness. Before I retired, I worked at the Stack Pole and Craddock Terry Shoe Factory as a machine operator in Farmville, Virginia where I lived. I also worked at McDonalds for one year in Baltimore, Maryland.

If school had not closed, when I graduated, I wanted to be an aide R.N. because I like working with people.

Alejia Pride -Carrington

 When Prince Edward County public schools closed in 1959, I was nine years old and had completed the fourth grade. Being so young, I can't remember how I found out about the

school closing; I could imagine when the fall came and I didn't go to school, my mother probably would have been the one to tell me that schools were not going to reopen. I am not sure if she would have said because of segregation or if she may have bluntly said to me "Because the white people don't want the blacks going to school with them." I don't remember how I felt when I heard it. I can only imagine at 9 years old I probably felt like it was an extended vacation.

When school closed, I went to Lunenburg County and was put out after thirty days because the school could not accommodate everybody who applied to attend. I had an older brother, an older sister and one younger brother also affected by the school closing. We played a lot, we read magazines like Sears Roebuck, Montgomery Ward, and whatever else we could find to read. We had aunts who lived in the north and they would occasionally send us boxes of clothing and books from the white families who didn't want them anymore. Other than the thirty days in Lunenburg County School, I received no formal education for four years. When school (The Free School) opened in 1963 I was 13. For the first time, I was going to ride a school bus; I was very frightened being bused from the small town of Meherrin, a little community called Virso. The bus took me to downtown Farmville to Mary E. Branch 2. I got off the bus to go in the school and someone yelled "If you are thirteen or older, get back on the bus. You are going to the high school". MORE FEAR! I was already frightened just riding a bus for the first time and now, after no school for four years, thirteen years old, I'm going to the high school. Once at the high school, students were grouped by age. I was placed in the 7th grade. At the end of the 7th grade, I was tested and placed in the 9th grade.

By the time, I reached my junior year, I felt tired and I did not want to be in school anymore. My senior year was awful. The only joy I had during my junior and senior years of high school was being with friends, but I didn't like school at all. During my senior year, I can't hide this, I missed 30 days. Ms. Vera Allen, Truant Officer/Guidance Counselor, visited my mother quite often. I had gotten to a point I just didn't want to go. I graduated from R. R. Moton in 1968. I was offered the opportunity to attend college. The offer was from an aunt who lived in Coatesville, Pennsylvania. She wanted me to attend Pennsylvania State. I said no, not having the desire to leave home or continue my education. To this day, I have no regrets.

I am happily retired from Sprint Telephone Company after thirty-one years of service. I was hired in 1971, making $1.70 an hour and my first raise was three cents. When I retired in 2002, I was making $17.50 an hour, which was a lot of money for this area.

I am totally happy with the life I have led. I never wanted to leave home, never had a desire to travel, and never imagined having lots of riches. After spending my childhood and some of my young adult life in rural Meherrin, Virginia, I now reside in Farmville, Virginia and loving it. When I leave Farmville, I want to leave in a box.

The closing of our public schools was quite frustrating. For years, I harbored much hatred, anger and anxiety. I personally don't think it should have happened. However, who am I to question God's will? I do believe it was His will. Now that I am older and have grown closer to God, I believe He allows everything to happen for a reason. I try not to question things that happen in my life anymore. Through prayer and God's love I no longer harbor the hatred, anger and anxiety I carried against the entire white race. My first public employment was with all people of the white race. I never acted on or spoke of the feelings I had for them, but I was always leery of being stabbed in the back. I always had in my mind that they hated me and nothing I did was good enough.

I had a good career with the phone company; those who did not like me being on the job with me, stayed to themselves. One employee, a young white man, left shortly after I was hired. I understand before I came, he said "Before I work with an N I will quit". He didn't quit! He was later transferred, but not because of me. I was told before he left, he told another employee that he had no idea black people could be intelligent. He had never worked with or been around any. He only knew the blacks who worked in the mills. We know mill workers were not ignorant. He was the one who was ignorant, by saying he would not work with me because of my skin color.

I do know I was hired at the telephone company because of my fair complexion. The law had passed for all public businesses to hire a minority and I believe I was the first fair skinned applicant and was expected to fail. However, I feel I was an asset to the company. I was offered management positions several times but refused because of family reasons and I did not wish to travel.

I am now spending my Golden Years with Perry, my husband of forty-two years. Our greatest joy is frequent visits with our three daughters and four grandchildren. God Is Good!

Frank Moseley

 I was in the ninth grade when school closed. I don't remember how I found out about the schools being closed. I didn't go anywhere; I stayed home and did odd and end jobs. The summer of 1963, I left the state of Virginia and went to New Jersey and worked in a summer camp for girls. When school reopened, I stayed in New Jersey working at the summer camp. Between breaks from the job and after camp was over, I lived in New Jersey with relatives. I don't know what I would have been or done if school had not closed. It may have changed some things if I had an education, my life might have been different, maybe it was for the best, the way my life turned out. Now I am retired after working for 39 years in construction doing carpentry, concrete finishing, masonry and dry wall on residential and commercial businesses.

George E. Davis

When school closed, I was in the eighth grade, I passed to the ninth. I didn't find out about it until the summer on the radio. At that time, I didn't know what to think, a lot of my friends left me behind right here in Farmville, so I didn't know what to think. When school closed, I stayed here in Farmville, I worked for Buffalo Shook for 7 or 8 years and I left and went to Stack Pole and then, I ran my own business, Davis Restaurant in 1994 on 460 at Prospect, Virginia.

When school reopened, I kept working, I was married then. I am retired from Stack Pole. If school had not closed what would I have done? - I really don't know, I often wonder about that, but I really don't know. I just got caught up, so I just let it go at that. I use to have bitterness about it, but not now, I don't' have it now.

Evelyn Antonette Saunders

I was only six years old when school closed. I was supposed to have gone to school that year when school closed. I found out about school closing because my mother was housekeeping and she was working for white family and that's how we found out. When I heard about it, I was upset because I was all excited about starting school for the first time. When school closed, I didn't do anything. I went with my mother to work every day. When school reopened, I was in the sixth grade, but my mother had taught me a lot, so I knew you know my ABC's and numbers and everything that I needed, just about what I needed to know to go into the sixth grade. When school opened, I attended Mary E. Branch 2, I stayed in school and graduated at Prince Edward High School in '71. Now I am a retired cook from Colonial Williamsburg, retired, disabled cook for 18 years and then I retired and had to go on disability.

Edward Hatcher, Jr.

I was in the eleventh grade when school closed. I found out about the school closing on the radio news. When I heard that school had closed, my reaction was where in the world was I going to go to school, I was poor.

When school closed, I stayed in Farmville, I got a job, I was supposed to go to Kittrell, but my mother couldn't afford it. My aunt was going to do it, but my mother said well, who is going to be here with me? I had five brothers, I was the oldest, I was five years older than my next brother, so I was like the babysitter and they had to work, so she said maybe next year, next year didn't 'come and by the next year, I was like, then well I didn't have but one more year and I felt that I had accomplished what I could learn in school. That's what I thought then, you know. At seventeen, I said well, how much more they are going to teach me and so I went out and got a job, and when school didn't open up, I got a girlfriend. I had to go to work then, to take care of her and the new baby.

When school reopened, I was working in Atlantic City, New Jersey in '64. I did not come back. Now I am retired from the Army Air force Exchange Services, which is an agency which serves the military. I retired there after 28 years. What would I have done or been if school had not closed? I have thought about that many times over the years, what I would have done. When I was in school, I had planned to go to college. I was hoping to go to college and I wanted to be a doctor. I had big dreams. Yea I did, I wanted to be a doctor. I would like to add that after I grew up, because when school closed, I was kid, I thought I was grown, but I was angry because I realized that the school closing turned my life upside down. Because during that time I was a real good student and I loved going to school and was B+ average A....and I could have done a lot of things in life, I know now, then so I was really angry about it, so when I was 35, I was living in Maryland and I had contacted some people about suing the board of education, yea, they took my life away. You know they shut the schools down. They said that a few people here (in Prince Edward County) had contacted them and they said it was impossible, because those racist pigs, (snickering) they burned up all the records, so it was no proof of who was in the schools. Did you know that? They said it would be hard to sue them because you couldn't prove that you were in school and what grades you were in; all the records were destroyed from the school. Yes, so that was all I could do, but still it was such a tragedy.

I understood it later, during the 60's, the revolution that they called it, when I got to meet people like Stokely Carmichael and H. Rap Brown and they were preaching in Washington D.C. My eyes was real open to a lot of things in history. Like I always thought the way for poor people and I realized that they were "Disocrats" and not democrats. Yea, I got to meet the Black Mayor of D.C. and the infamous mayor of D.C, I got to meet him, I got to meet Jessie Jackson in 69, and Reverend Shuttleworth. I participated in D.C. during the march and I got to hear Martin Luther King. A friend and I went, we couldn't get to the mall, but his sister's house was near the mall, we looked at it from her porch and we watched it on TV, after that I worked with the poor people campaign in D.C. All the poor people came with their goats, mules, and set up tents on the National Park in D.C. They called it the Poor People's Campaign. They came to show how poor people were. Most of them came from the South. That helped the voter movement that is when the food stamps came along. I have done a lot of work trying to help out. I knocked on doors to get people sign up for food stamps when that first came out.

First, I worked with the George McGovern campaign during 1968 when Robert Kennedy died. He came to D.C. I saw Robert Kennedy two weeks before he was killed. The people that were working for that campaign, when we found out that he was going to run, we started working for the Robert Kennedy campaign. I started working for the George McKinney campaign. It made me real political, you know. I had been working with voter registration, but I lived in Europe for two years, so I was out of the mainstream America. I was going to stay in Europe, but when I heard about Barrack Obama running for president, I came back and worked for his campaign until he was voted in. Even the day of the campaign, I was canvassing; we went to Pennsylvania Election Day. Yea I worked a lot for political campaigns, I worked canvas, calling canvassing.

I did a lot and believe it or not, I hate to say this, I was a militant during 66's and the school closing here really drove me to be that way, because I just got mad. You know, as the years went by, I was struggling, I got my GED, but still I realized that living in D.C. if I had a degree, like the jobs I could have gotten, but just the normal jobs and it made me angrier and angrier. So I felt like the only thing I could do anything about what happened here, was understand how it happened. After Reverend Griffin, we didn't have any leaders. It just didn't just happen here, in the United States we were promised to get an education and I couldn't understand how the governor let Prince Edward County do what they wanted to in Virginia. The school that closed in one side of Charlottesville, but they sent the kids to the other side, so the kids weren't affected in that school, because the black kids had transferred to another school.

I stayed angry for years about it. I am truly not still angry, but I feel cheated. I always tell my kids, I was the type of person, right today I can say, I don't know what I would have been had school stayed open and I graduate from college. You know, I know life would have been easier. In all and all life wasn't that hard for me, but I did get a GED, I did get lucky, I would say and got into the department of civilian force by working for the government. I had a chance to start working my way up from a laborer to an assistant manager to a retail manager. I had to go to school. I started out working customer service, and retail, that's what I did, they had their own manager company, in the Air Force Exchange Services. I had to go to Europe to get any decent job. I didn't want to cut pulp wood, and I went to Europe and life got a whole lot better, I tried, but I couldn't have gotten it in the United States at that time. This was in 1977. I know it was a blessing. I left Farmville to find a better life; I went to New York and had my 19th birthday. I was working here making $20.00 a week, went to New York, and did get up to $45.00 a week.

I went to D.C for two years, I drove a taxi for 10 years, a lot of things I learned from them, picking up people from the airport and that is what got me interested, I picked up a German one night and he said have you ever thought about going to Germany? To me Germany at that time was Nazis, I said no, he said you should try it, it's nice over there, we care about our people, we take care of our people and they have social medicine. That's the reason I liked it there, because you paid taxes, but everybody had medical, if you worked or even if you didn't work, you had to have free medical, it was health care, everybody had healthcare, and I worked, after working nine months you had 6 weeks' vacation a year. Yea, they looked out for family, because they knew you could go away on vacation and for spring before vacation time, they got a bonus from the job, I think it was 15% of your pay, they gave you extra money for vacation. I was getting about $900 and then for Christmas everybody got 29% of their salary. You know, so they helped people live, and life was good. But when I was in Baltimore I drove taxi for 5 years, the only way, those times, like I said, I was still mad and I couldn't work- and taxi I drove, you didn't have to work for anybody, so it was dangerous, but I did it because I didn't want to work for the white man, that's all. Although they owned the taxi, they leased it to me, so I made my money and paid them and I kept mine. I learned a lot during those years.

I came back and worked for two years. It was still the same, working for Longwood College and Hamden Sydney College, working for their food service or either with Buffalo Shook, so I stayed away from there.

Gregory Hicks

 I was in the 5th grade at Mt. Leigh School in Green Bay, Virginia when school closed. We were made aware of the school closing by my parents, and the talk of the neighborhood. I was disappointed and hurt. I would be limited to farm chores daily.

I attended free school at High Rock Baptist Church in Rice, Virginia when it was formed. When I got my driver's license Mr. Whitt Paige asked my dad and I about driving the school bus for that area. I accepted. I would pick up the students and take them to High Ridge Baptist Church and also to High Rock Baptist Church and pick up lunch for Warsaw School at Meherrin, Virginia, and return to take the students home. When schools reopened, I was placed in the 9th grade and quickly to the 10th. I was eager to learn.

I presently operate and manage a trucking business. We move pre-case concrete to various locations for parking garages and buildings in Virginia, Maryland, Delaware, Pennsylvania and West Virginia. We had hands on experience with the parking deck at Liberty University, Lynchburg, Virginia in 2014. I wanted to be a professional race car driver or a lawyer. My dad wanted me to be a lawyer. God had other plans; school closed.

I am thankful that I was able to graduate. I wasn't able to go away to school when they closed like some of my siblings. When I graduated in 1968, I moved to New Jersey where I had brothers and sisters and other family. I got a job at Nabisco, a cookie factory. I went to school part time studying machine shop at Patterson Tech, Patterson, New Jersey. I later changed to a truck diagnostic job at Paramus, N.J. In 1970, I answered an ad for a driver over the road delivery. It required experience and to be 25 years of age. I was 22 and had only experience for farming and logging equipment. I guess by then my boss liked me or what I did because the tenured driver was having truck trouble that I could fix, so I got hired. He was going to take a chance on me with the insurance; I thanked him, and said to him, "I'll try for you not to regret it." That job was very educational. I had to do invoices, handle checks and cash. This was great in that I wanted to travel. Being a delivery and relay driver enabled me to travel the area between Savanna, Georgia to the Canadian Border and East to Mississippi River with the exception of Maine. We were based out of Elizabeth, N.J.

In 1982, I formed G. Hicks Enterprises doing various hauling. We then located to Virginia in 1985. We constructed and opened a convenience store in 1990. My wife and I operated this along with the trucking business until 1999. Our son was born in 1996. This got to be more than what we wanted to do. We closed the store and I continued to operate the trucking business. In 1994, I incorporated and accepted a contract with Richfood, now Super Value between the Carolinas and Pennsylvania and New Jersey until 2006. The name change eliminated outside contractors. I then contracted with Tindall Corporation based at Spartanburg, S.C. I work out of the Virginia Division where I am at present, in Petersburg, Virginia.

Certainly, the school closing affected my course. I guess

most youngsters has dreams and wants, however; God had different plans. I am blessed to have been able to graduate and thankful to have traveled the pathway of life that I have, for it is his guidance and Blessing that has enabled me to be where I am. This is an example of how the enemy set a stumbling block before you for a hindrance and God turned it into a Blessing. Thank you, Lord, thank you. Truly I am.

Larry L. Jordan

When school closed, I would have been going to the first grade. I found out about the school closing from my parents. I didn't know what to think. I really did not understand. I think my parents and grandparents sheltered me from a lot of the negative things that was going on. My father worked for the Railroad and my mother was a homemaker and later went to work at a local factory.

I went to a training school for two years in Prospect, VA. After that, I attended schools in Appomattox County because of a scheme my grandparents worked out. They rented an old house and we pretended to live there while my parents transported us daily. I did not realize how much my parents and grandparents sacrificed for me until later in life.

When school re-opened, I returned to Prince Edward County. I was in the 5th grade. I was skipped two grades. Now I am retired from Norfolk and Western Railroad after 29 years. Also spent 3 years in the U.S. Army. I always wanted to be a State trooper and I took test after graduating high school. Three Black guys took the test on the same day. We were all told that we failed. Rather than give up and do nothing, I volunteered for the military.

I found out that the discrimination was deeper than the closing of schools. There were a lot of missed opportunities. After not being accepted by the Virginia state trooper, I joined the Army. After being in the army for a while two federal agents came to see me. I was alarmed when I was told that the agents were waiting to see me because I could not imagine what they wanted. They told me that they had investigated a discrimination complaint and found that I had passed the state trooper examine. I was told that I could return and work as a state trooper when I got out of the military. I often wonder how my life would have been different, if discrimination had not blocked my opportunity to be a state trooper.

Jerry Smith

When school closed, I passed from the 4th to the 5th grade. I found out about the school closing from reading it in the paper, the Farmville Herald. How I felt about the school closing, I guess the word now would be dumb founded. You know it's something that you look forward to and summer of the year and then fall of the year you look forward to going to school. After school closed, I went to a little school in Cumberland, it was back in the woods somewhere. I think the name of the school was Hawks, something like that. I only went for about a month. They had outdoor toilets and all there too, so I just came on back home on Bridge Street.

When school reopened, I went back to school and I had a paper route at that time, I was carrying the Richmond News Leaders in the evening and nothing much until I got in the high school. When I went back to school, they put me back in the 5th grade, I took a test, I passed the test, instead of putting me in the 6th grade, I went to the 7th and at the end of that year, I took another test, what they called the Scholastic Test and I went from the 7th to the 9th, so I made up all of my years that way. I graduated at 18 in 1968.

I am retired now. I retired from the Town of Farmville, but I worked 14 years for Atlantic and Pacific which is the A& PT Company and after they closed, I went to Powhatan at Deep Meadow Prison for a year, and while I was there an opening came to Par Bills, which was a local convenience store and I came to work at Par Bills and I worked there for 20 years, I managed that at night. I left there and went to the Regional Jail for about 6 months, I wasn't no prisoner (laugh) I was an officer up there and I didn't like it, so I came back to Par-Bills. By that time, they had sold out to a foreigner and I worked for him for about 6 months, but during that time, I was on Town Council. I had won the election and I was on Town Council for four years while I was on Town Council and after I got defeated, I got a job with the town and I put in 7 years with the town and then I retired.

If school had not closed, for some reason I always wanted to be a lawyer, (smile) because I could set and figure out a lot of stuff for people and right now, I still do a lot of things helping people out in the community.

The closing of the schools was a real hindrance to a lot of people, a lot of us were affected. You look at people today and some of them that didn't go back to school, had great minds, could do a lot of things, great football players and all, but that closing of the schools just affected them and it tore a lot of families apart because it separated their kids from their parents and they really didn't get the, when you miss that mother and father, their love, can't anybody else give that to you. They can try, but they can't give it to you like mama and daddy can.

Rosa Marie Johnson-Bedford

I was in the second grade when school closed. It was just when it was time for school to get ready to open up, our parents told us that school was closed. When I heard that school was closed, my feeling was, what we going to do? When school closed, I didn't go nowhere. I stayed at home the whole five years because I was the oldest girl and we didn't go anywhere because mama couldn't afford to send us anywhere.

When school reopened, I went to Mary E. Branch #2 School. We walked up there, my brothers and sisters and I walked up to Branch 2 from Watkins Street and back every day. I continued going to school in Prince Edward, I dropped out in 68. I had two sons and I went back to school and got my high school diploma at Robert R. Moton High School. I graduated in 1973, Mr. William Penn was my principal at the time.

Right now, well I was working at Prince Edward County Public School as an In-School Suspension Coordinator. I worked at Prince Edward for 14 years. Before then I worked for Rehab for like 20 years and now, I stopped working and retired to take care of my husband, he had a stroke.

If school had not closed, I was planning on being an RN, but I did go to school and get my CNA license and I am still certified as a CNA. When I graduated in 1973, I went on and furthered my education in rehab and a CNA. In the year 1999, I tried to sign up to become a Home Economics Teacher, but they weren't offering that course anymore. Right now, as of today, 2009, I was licensed as a Minister of the Gosper.

The closing of the school affected so many people and a lot of the students didn't go back. It was real hard for them because the parents of the ones that didn't go back and some of the kids didn't learn anything.

What might it feel like finding a way to continue your child's education by pretending to live in an abandoned or rented house in another county to attend school, only to find out a portion of the house was in Prince Edward County? Several children will tell their experiences of how their parents found innovative solutions in order for them to attain an education.

Doris Robinson -Brown

 I was in the eighth grade when school closed. I found out about school closing by really the word of mouth, people in the neighborhood talking upset because now I had to work on the farm harder (laughing). After school was closed, my mother rented a house in Appomattox along with another family. The house for some reason was surveyed. They discovered that the sleeping quarters was in Prince Edward County, so Appomattox about its not going to be any schools. When I heard that school had closed, I was very upset the County put us out of school. After that my mother became acquainted with the Quakers and my sister and I were sent to Barea, Kentucky to attend the high school program.

When school reopened, I came back to Prince Edward County to the Free School. I was going into the 12th grade. I graduated from Prince Edward County Free School. Right now, I am retired from the Prince Edward County Sheriff Department.

Andrew Hill

I was in the fifth grade when school closed. I found about the school closing, well, we heard it at school and everybody talking about it. Some people were happy, we were so young, we didn't realize it meant no education until we had to stay at home. They made us work harder at home than when we were in school. We were ready to go back to school then. When I found out that school was closed, we had mixed feelings then, some of us were happy, and then again when it was time to go back to school, we were, it kind of bothered me.

After we stayed out for a year, mother and father, we got together with other cousins and family and we found another house and rented a house in another county and went to school at Carver Price, Appomattox, Virginia. Carver Price then because all schools were named after black people then. It was eight or ten kids, each week one parent would stay and make sure the kids would eat, make sure we got our homework, make sure we got up to go to school and got dressed, did everything like they supposed to, and they supervised us, we had chores to do, everybody got along great. All of us was cousins, you know, about eight kids in the same house, a four-room house, we did good.

We went to another school, all of us were hungry for an education, all of us did so good, and some of the kids in other schools looked like they were kind of jealous because we going to school, was doing so much better and the teacher expected more of them. We got up there, we went on through it like a breeze, like the school standards wasn't as high as Prince Edward.

We stayed there until school reopened in Prince Edward, came back, graduated at R.R. Moton in 1967 and I drove the school bus. I got drafted in the army 1968 and left home, got out of the army in 1970, came back home, had the opportunity to work on the railroad, my father was there. I got a job as a brakeman, but I am young and wild and what happen, I went down and tried out and qualified for the job as a brakemen, but they put you on call, I was young, you know, I said I was not going to be on call, I say I am not going to stay at home all the time and wait for a call, so I left and worked in a foundry in Lynchburg, Virginia. Got a job there working three days and they went on strike. I wasn't in the union, so I wasn't going to walk out of the building, they told me to walk out of the building because you might get hurt, so I walked out.

I had a cousin that came down from New Jersey that weekend, I told my mother I'm going up north, got in the car that Sunday, went to New Jersey and stayed with my cousin that night. My cousin in New York picked me up Monday morning, took me to White Plains, New York. My cousin husband or somebody went down to General Motors, on a Monday and I went to work on Tuesday in Tarrytown, New York. Worked there for about two or three months and got laid off. I came to Patterson, New Jersey in 1970, while I'm laid off, I ran into my cousin and all my friends from Virginia, family and friends, Gregory Hicks, John Hicks, all of them worked in Nabisco, and what happened, they said you looking for a job man? I said yea. They said come to Nabisco, they hiring. I went out there on Thursday, went to work on Monday and stayed there for 35 years and that was it.

I even went to school then at a college while I was working to Passaic County Community College for business in Patterson, New Jersey. I was working full time at a bakery and then I got married in 1986. My wife got real sick in 95, she didn't work no more. I kept working until 2005 and she got worse, so I went on and retired to take care of her. In 2007 I got a house in North Carolina and stayed there seven years, sold the house in Patterson and she was really ill and passed in 2013. I got rid of the house and came back home in Prince Edward County.

If school had not closed? Well at that age I didn't really know what I wanted to do, because after I went into the army as military police, they had a program if you got excepted at the police department, you could get out of the army early, so I had told my mother about it, but she didn't want me to be a police at that time. I was young, in the army, I didn't argue with her, so I say send me the papers from Farmville to be a police and stuff, but I didn't follow up with it. So I stayed in there and made the best of it and came home when I got out. I worked at Nabisco, but when I retired it was Kraft Foods, unskilled labor. I was the line attendant reliever. Worked on line to make sure the machine was working right, put the paper in, I was like a carton cutter. I would relieve other guys so they could go on break. When one come back from a half hour lunch, I would relieve another one, because the line never stops, never shuts the line down, I let the man go and when he came back, let another leave, that's all I did, it was good, it was good times. I don't think school should have closed. It was hard on a lot of people. I was very fortunate to be able to go to school and didn't have to stay out four or five years, you know, I was really blessed.

Vonita White - Foster

 I had completed third grade at Mary E. Branch Elementary School when PEC closed public schools. My parents told me and my siblings about closing of schools. They also shared with us the plan for us to continue our education. We would be leaving our home and parents to attend school in other state, Baltimore, Maryland.

My reaction to the news was tears flowing down my face. My heart was broken and I was afraid. Also, I was filled with questions. I asked questions and my parents answered. We would be living our small town and moving to a big city. I was a nervous and unhappy! I told my parents I was not leaving.

I had four siblings: Darwyn (deceased), Reginald, Jacqueline, and Debra and we would be attending a private school, St. Edwards Catholic School, in Baltimore, Maryland. We were separated from parents and each other. My parents remained in Farmville, Virginia. I lived with my grandparents with my sister Jacqueline. My oldest sister, Darwyn, and my youngest sister, Debra, lived with an aunt. My brother, Reginald, lived with another aunt. We attended St. Edwards for two years and only saw each other in school. After two years, we attended public schools in Cumberland County, Virginia. My parents decided to bring us back home and rented a house in neighboring Cumberland County. We lived in our home in Farmville, but were driven by our father to the empty rental home in Cumberland each morning. We were picked up after school.

We attended PEC Free School Association the fifth year of the public-school closures. When public schools opened, we enrolled. I was in the 8th grade. I have had diverse opportunities in my career. I earned two Masters Degrees. One in Library Science and another in Education Administration and Supervision. I continued my studies and received a terminal degree, a Doctor of Philosophy Degree in Education. My professional career began at the Library of Virginia, the state library for the Commonwealth of Virginia. I also was employed at three different institutions of higher education, and a fortune 500 company. Moreover, I was the Executive Director of the U. S. National Slavery Museum. Currently, I work for a public-school system. I've always wanted to help children and young adults excel in education and to become lifelong learners.

The only affect the closing of public schools had on my son is disbelief and astonishment that such an unthinkable event could happen in America.

I pursued and was awarded four degrees and continue daily to learn something new every day. I embrace learning 4 life. I think my thirst for education was because of what occurred in PEC, Virginia to Black children and families. Moreover, what happened, I believe, left a deep scar in the hearts and minds of all PEC citizens of all colors and creed. The scab is healing, but I truly believe it is bleeding slowly and will not completely heal until PEC does something to rectify its ugly past. Moreover a few of my classmates, family members and friends began a foundation to help students attending the only high school in PEC. The Lest We Forget Foundation was established in 2005. Our mission is to assist children of students who were directly affected by the PEC closing of public schools in 1959-1964. We have provided college scholarships to 10 students, and provided assistance to students to help with textbooks and supplies while in college.

Dale Lee

 I was in the second grade when school closed. I heard about the school closing through my parents. I was very sad. My mother was a school teacher, so we were home schooled for the first two years after school closed. And then my father rented some property across Cumberland Bridge and then we end up going to a school called Hawk School, a one room school. It's some other building now, but the structure was still there. You had to be a resident to go to Cumberland school, so he rented a house and he drove us there every morning and dropped us off at that house on a property. We didn't live in it, we rented it, but it had no furniture in it, the only thing that was in it was a wood stove and during the winter we would put wood in the wood stove and use it for heat until the bus came. When school reopened, I came back here to Prince Edward County to the Free School. I was in the 8th grade when school reopened. I graduated from Prince Edward County High School in 1971.

Now I am a curator for an art gallery in San Francisco, California. If school had not closed, my alternate goal would have either been a school teacher or a registered nurse. I just wish the younger generation knew more about the school closing and were educated on it and realize how important education is and what people went through in order for them to obtain an education then.

Dorothy Holcomb

 I completed the 4th grade when school closed. I actually found out from my father about the school closing. He just came home one afternoon and told us. I don't know if he had been to a meeting or not but he told me that schools were not going to reopen. I felt an overwhelming sense of sadness. I loved school and I didn't want not to go school. After schools closed, initially I went to the basement of the Methodist Church in Prospect and we were tutored there by one of our former teachers, Mrs. Beatrice Davenport. She did that for us and I went there for two years and after that school didn't open so we went to school in Appomattox County.

My parents thought they would try to wait it out initially and just do the best they could and let us go to the training center in Prospect. After that didn't work out and our parents did not want to separate us and send us out of state to live with anybody else, so we stayed at home and went to the church for two years and then we went to Appomattox County where we rented an old house and pretended we lived there and we went to school there. The Free school opened in Prince Edward and then my parents decided to stay in Appomattox County. I finished school in Appomattox. I had two brothers and one brother did not go back to school at all after the training center deal, but the other one, Edward and I went to Appomattox, and we stayed. I was a ninth grader when schools reopened in Prince Edward. I graduated in Appomattox County at Carver Price High School.

Imagine in that era, a Black child taken from their community and normal environment to be placed in the homes of white families in order to attend school. Here are their stories.

James E. Lee, Jr.

I was in the 10th grade when school closed in 1959. I found out about the school closing through word of mouth around town. When I heard about the school closing, I didn't believe it and I was devastated, because I loved school. I had so many records from not being tardy and absent and I was an honor roll student. When school closed, the first year I didn't go to school. Closing of the schools was heart breaking and just caught us off guard. We heard it, but we didn't believe it. It caught us off guard and we didn't have any money, so we didn't have anywhere to go and my mother couldn't send us anywhere and that's when we were contacted by the American Services Committee. My sisters went to Luther P. Jackson High School in Cumberland, Virginia, but once they found out that they didn't live in Cumberland, they could no longer go, and then they went under the same program I went in Massachusetts.

I was contacted through Reverend Griffin by the American Friends City Committee. Because of being angry about the school closing, I wanted to go the furthest from Virginia I could and I chose Iowa City, Iowa. I didn't know a soul there, but I wanted to go just to get away from Virginia. I stayed there from 1961- 1962. I graduated from Iowa City

High School in1962. The only thing about it was that I couldn't make the honor roll. There were two colleges in Iowa City, Iowa University and Iowa State College and when you got a college in the city that you go to high school in high school and middle school were much tougher and it was nothing compared to Prince Edward. Like I said, I could enroll through Prince Edward, but I couldn't enroll through the school of Iowa. I graduated, but I didn't graduate with honors. If I had stayed at Prince Edward, I could have.

When I went to Iowa City High school there were only two blacks in the whole school and they were sisters. I wasn't mistreated, but I was asked a lot of questions I was interviewed like I am doing now. People were coming from everywhere wanting to know what Farmville was like, wanting to know the same questions. I couldn't go to church unless they was standing on the steps taking pictures; took pictures in school, took pictures in church, took pictures when I went to the grocery store. I was never left alone. They were there all the time and I was in the paper all the time. The first year me, Otis Wiley and James Brown went together, but they refused to go back the second year. They didn't like it because there were too many white people. So instead of them going, James Ghee went. James Ghee stayed there, graduated, and attended college. I left him there after I graduated. He came behind me, he came as a junior high, I think it was 9th or 10th grade, but I liked it there. I stayed with two white families. The first family was the Michaelson and the last family was the Midlons and I enjoyed it very much.

I got to come home only one time a year and that was Christmas. Both families have been here to visit me. From 1962-2013, I get a Christmas and Birthday gift, my birthday is in December so I get a Birthday and Christmas gift from the Midlons every year. The man died, but the lady is still living. They sent me so many nice sweaters and shirts, so last year I wrote a nice letter and told her I had so many, would she send me cash instead. Last year she sent me a $100 check.

I had already graduated when school reopened in Prince Edward. Now I work as an attendant at a laundry mat. I have been there for 14 years, they call it Bubble Mat Coin Laundry.

If school had not closed I always wanted to be a teacher, but when school closed it was devastating and I just lost interest in everything. So when I came out of school, I went to work and have been working ever since, because after I graduated I went to school at First Baptist Church basement in Farmville for a while, they were having classes and you would go to churches and places to teach adults. I taught at First Rock Adult classes in Prospect, Virginia, Lillian Blanton and I were teaching adult people how to read. I did that for two years and that was nice. We had to take classes at First Baptist before we could do that. The kid's classes were called Head Start and I forgot what the adult classes were called.

I set aside hatred and got into the church and everything and I forgive these people. At the time it was a whole lot of segregation, but it's not as much now as it used to be.

When I was growing up 15, 16 years old, I had a whole lot of hatred for white people because I knew they were the ones who did it, wasn't personally did it, but they was all working together, and I was holding animosity in my heart, but I finally got rid of it. I finally got rid of it, because I'm trying to make Heaven my home and I can't carry hatred in my heart for what they have done, because you got to be forgiving.

I say to anybody that got a chance to go to school, please go, stay in, graduate and if you can go further, go further, but don't jump out of school because you don't like school, say school is boring, but you have the opportunity to go. We didn't have that opportunity. For five years school was closed, a lot of people got a chance to go away, but it may not happen again. My mother was doing days' work for white people on High Street. We had to stay at home by ourselves, with no company and we couldn't leave the yard, and we just read books, playing and watching TV and listening to the radio at night and it wasn't nothing like being in a classroom. We won't learning anything, we was just passing away time until this program came about and I thank God today for Reverend L. Frances Griffin and the American Friends Services Committee from I think Pennsylvania.

Phyllistine Ward-Mosley

 I was in the 10th grade when school closed. I found out about the school closing in spring 1959 when I really realized we may not be coming back to school in fall of 59' when our basketball coach Miss Malone said "to clean out our lockers". There was no talk around with the students that we would not be back to Moton in the fall.

My reaction was not much because all of the talk around us was where would we be going to school. The summer of 59' was spent at vacation school at First Baptist Church in Farmville, traveling to New York for vacation, the Prince Edward Lake and then we finally realized there was talk about us going to school in N.C. I did not realize at that time that we were heading off to "boarding school" but that was my brother Ronald Ward and several cousins, Alfred Reid and Ralph Smith would be together at the high school.

After school closed, I attended Kittrell Junior College (2-year high school program), Kittrell North Carolina. In 1959-1960, I completed the 11th grade at Kittrell. We were juniors at Kittrell and did not want to miss out on school activities and events that we would have done if we were still at home going to our school, so we pushed for a Jr/Sr prom, cheerleaders, football teams, choir and all of the activities we could. Since it was a two-year college program, we experienced what would be like going to college too. So, we made the best of being away from home and family, we missed home a lot, but always looked forward to the "boxes" from home which had food, snack and clothing. My brother Ronald graduated from Kittrell. That was a great day to see all of our families come to NC and see our senior do the graduation march through the campus.

In 1960-1961 the American Friends Service came to Farmville offering the opportunity for students to attend school in the North and mid-west. Parents had to sign up for this and allow their child to be even further away from home. I enjoyed my junior year at Kittrell, but I was adventurous and this was a chance for me to see another part of the country and meet different people. The concern I had was, would I be able to come back home for Christmas and my parents attend my graduation. Was not sure if we could do all of that with a brother Gerald at St. Paul's College and my sister Betty still at home in school living with my grandparents. I did not know whom I had been settled to live with.

There were six of us that traveled to Yellow Springs, Ohio to live with three Quaker families and three black families. I am not sure how we were selected to live with whom but the choices were great, I got to live my senior year with a Quaker family with four children, Rebecca, Charlie, Douglas and Julia Ruopp and mother Frankie and father Phillip Ruopp. Mr. Ruopp was a professor at Antioch College and the mother was a homemaker. It was a perfect match for me and I just fitted into the family. I did have to adjust to some of the meals she cooked especially the hot tuna casserole. School was great and we got a lot of support from the school and community. We had our own bikes to get around the small village of Yellow Springs. (I traveled back there in 2003 for the memorial service of Frankie Roupp and the village had not changed much). I have kept close contact with the Ruopp family since living with them.

When school re-opened, I had finished high school in 1961 and enrolled at Bennett College in Greensboro, N.C. 1961-1965. I majored Home Economics which my high school teacher Mrs. Minnie Miller influenced me while I was in the 9th and 10th grade at Prince Edward County Moton High. I worked for the Virginia Cooperative Extension Service 1961-1996 and retired. I have a Master Degree from VA Tech in Adult Education; I am now a professional volunteer. I serve on several boards and the Legacy Museum of African American History. Currently, I had the opportunity to serve on the Brown v Board Education Scholarship Commission appointed by former Gov. Mark Warner.

Retired since 1996, I travel, enjoy having family times with children Sam and Kim and five grandchildren. My oldest grandson Phillip is a freshman at Lincoln University which Fred Ward attended. I ran and was elected for the Campbell County Robert E. Lee Soil and Water District as Director for the past four years. My husband Sam was delegate to the 2012 Democrat Convention and I got to travel with him and very active with the Democratic Committee.

If school had not closed, I would have done the same things, go to college, get a job, get married and have children and volunteer to make a difference in my community and the lives of families. The only difference is that we were denied the opportunity to grow up with our family and experience the family life we would have had together if we could have continued school in our home town of Farmville, VA, There are so many activities and events we could have shared together as I experienced with my children during their high school years.

Having to leave home for an education was not my choice; my families would not allow their children to leave home which was a hardship for both us our families. Both Black and White had to cope with the situation and deal with the unknown for five years too long. Thanks to the leadership of Rev. Griffin and the law we were able to have our school reopen for the children.

We don't know all of the stories, but the ones we do are unreal for some. I am now meeting folks who lived in Farmville during that time and they don't want to talk about it. One lady said they moved to Farmville when the school closed. Asked why and she said" his job moved him there and they went to the private school.

Annie Marie Barksdale-Rice

I was in the 6th grade when school closed. I found out that school was closed when some social workers told us. I was 15, we didn't understand what was going on. Robert Ellis, a neighbor, use to take us around and a lot of us were at different people house singing and cheering. He was our chauffeur and take us around so all of us could get together and sing, we needed to be free. Social Services came and talked to some of the parents, they got us to go away. The first time I went away was to Dayton, Ohio. I stayed with a white family, Mr. and Mrs. Lumback. I went to school up there, but the first year when school was closed, I couldn't go because my father got hurt, and I had to stay and take care of the little kids, but my brothers went, so I was the only one who stayed at home.

The rest of my family, we really were affected. I didn't even get to finish school. It really hurt me when I found out that school had closed, because I really wanted to go to school, because I really wanted to be a teacher. So that really did mess things up and then when we came back home, we had to take care of our mom, my brothers, my family, we didn't get to go. When school reopened, I came back, but by that time I was 18 years old and I didn't feel like sitting in class with little kids and I was way older than them, so I just dropped out.

Now I am retired from Hamden Sydney College. I worked in the president's house for over 20 some years, taking care of the family and I was in charge (laugh). If school had not closed, I wanted to be a secretary or a teacher, because I love people and I love talking. I thank God, we did get back and everybody could go back to school and everybody that wanted to go, they went on and they are happy about it and I am happy that they went on back, so now I am telling my children that anything that you can do, do it, don't waste no time because I feel bad because I didn't finish. So, I want them to get every opportunity, go for it, don't break no records. Do what you need to do for your family.

I have three sons and one is an engineer in Dallas, the other one is a boss in Texas, and the other one has his own business and my daughter, she takes care of patients in their home and another daughter was working at Hampden Sydney College, in the dining room, but she has health problems all the time, so I am staying close to her to make sure she is ok. I am hanging in there and I thank God to be where I am today, because if it wasn't for him, I wouldn't be here. You got to have faith and keep on pushing. I don't let nothing get me down, I am happy. I don't blame anybody, because thats over with and my son married a white girl and I love her just as well as I love the rest of them. I got no problem with that, because I love everybody.

A few children had to return home shortly after leaving because a family member became ill. When hearing these stories, I often wonder if their emotional state factored into some of these illnesses. If it was possible, that from being tormented by the fact that their child was away from them, living with strangers and not knowing how they will be treated; somehow triggered their illnesses. Here is one telling her story.

Marjorie West-Jones

I was in the 6th grade when school closed. I found out that school had closed from the neighborhood, from Anna and all of my aunts told us, because we were at home and my mother said we couldn't go back to school because school was closed. When I heard that school was closed, I felt terrible at the time, I felt really terrible, because I was looking forward to going back to school, because I loved school. When school closed, the first year, I didn't go anywhere, the second year, I went to Luther P. Jackson for a year and a half and then I had to go back home and stay with my aunt in Cumberland and then my mother got sick and I had to come back home and help with her, because my other two sisters had left home and gotten jobs in New York, and I was the next oldest one, so I had to go back home.

When school reopened, I went back to school, my sister who had just started and my brother went back to school. They put me in the 10th grade; I went to R.R. Moton High School and the others went to the elementary. I stayed in school until we got out for Christmas, I did not go back in January, I felt too old; I stayed at home and I went on and got a job. I had a lot of jobs. I worked at the Craddock Terry Shoe Factory, I worked at the Cedar Brook Restaurant, and got a job at Stack Pole, I worked there for

10 years until it closed down then I went to Richmond and worked at E.R. Carpenters for about seven years and came back, I moved back and got a job at Thomasville Furniture Factory.

If school had not closed, I would have been a nurse. I always wanted to be a nurse; I could have been a RN. I could have been anything. I loved the way nurses dressed, that white uniform and those shoes, I just loved that. I tried to go back, but it was too late for me, but at that time, I probably could have done it. I should have gone back. I probably could have. I started ushering at church just to wear that uniform and those white shoes. I took nursing training, nurse's aide and worked for Personal Care and got a nursing assistance license.

I am retired now after 32 years from Thomasville Furniture Factory. It's so many things I want to say, but I don't know how to put it in words. I think it was a shame they closed our schools and there were so many children here in Prince Edward and myself that could have had beautiful jobs. I could have had a career; I don't know what I could have been, I could have been a doctor you know, it was a terrible shame, but never the less - forward. I learn to be grateful for it and I am going forward and that's it. (She could not talk about it anymore. I ended the interview because I could tell she was getting too emotional).

Going back to school after five years was not easy, particular for children who had become teenagers, 18 years or older. There were those who tried, but due to the classroom settings, could not adjust, therefore discontinued their education.

Earl (Yasin) Odom

"My brother was one-year younger, going away to school and leaving him behind left me with a broken heart and guilt throughout my adult life."

My brother Earl was in the 5th grade when school closed. He attended school when it reopened, but did not finish high school. Sadly enough, I can remember very little about him and where he was during the time we were separated, he stayed home and I was not told anything about my brother while I was away in school, and he and I never discussed it.

Two years before he passed, he came home and for the first time I decided to ask him what happened to him when schools were closed. His reply was shocking when I heard that he had been taken to Georgia by a couple of young teachers or students. Whether my mother understood that he would be there not to attend school, but to help with younger children, I will never know. I was too shocked to ask why he didn't go to school there. Maybe they saw that he was extremely smart, in spite of not being educated. My focus was always on the 40 years of pain I carried in my heart for leaving him behind.

He also told me that he had gotten his GED in Connecticut years later. I do know while we both were out of school before I left, each day he would go somewhere with books in his arms. I found out later he was going to an older lady's house to read to her, or maybe it was the other way around. I know he also had ties with the Griffins, Reverend L. Francis Griffin and his children, because he always talked about being over at their house and mentioning the children's names, but I never remembered him saying he attended the makeshift school in the basement of, First Baptist Church, many referred to as Reverend Griffin's Church.

He served in the United States Army and loved to read and owned so many comic books that neighborhood kids his age and much older would come almost daily to our house looking through or reading them. Even though a lot of his self-esteem had been damaged beginning with the closing of the school and life changes, he was a proud and a man of extraordinary intelligence. He once operated a home for troubled children in Ohio, had excellent reflexology skills and read numerology for people from different parts of the country from his home and on the computer in Maine. He has one daughter, and four sons who resides from Ohio, Maine to Colorado.

Joseph Johnson

I was 14 years old when school closed. The first year I stayed home and the next year I went to Appomattox to go to school and stayed until Free School opened in 1963. I came back for one year and quit because they wanted me to repeat the grade. I went to New York and worked in a factory until I became disabled. My twin brother stayed in Prince Edward County School and graduated.

Robert Douglas Carter

I was fourteen when school closed. I found out that school had closed because I felt disappointed. I felt that I wanted to get the education that I see a lot of other people going to school and I wanted to get the education.

When school closed, I didn't go anywhere, I stayed at home. When school opened, I went back to R. R Moton School, but I didn't complete it.

If school had not closed, well I tell you, I would have like to finish my education so I could, you know, have done some of the things I had in mind like getting a better job, you know. Back in that time you had to have an education to get a real good job. I am sorry school closed at that time. Now I am retired from Hampden Sydney College after 33 years.

Nellie Randolph -Sims

I was 14 years old when school closed. I found out about the school closing because I was in it. My reaction to the school closing was devastated,

I couldn't believe it. When school closed, I went to work babysitting. When Free School reopened, I was 18 years old and did not return back to school. I got married and had a family of my own. If school had not been closed, I would love to have been a school teacher. I was very upset when school closed, knowing that I couldn't finish my education. I am retired from Stackpole Carbone of America.

Michael Carter

I had just passed to the 6th grade when school closed. I found out that school was closed from everybody else and when it was time to go to school, the school was closed. In '59 when school closed down, I didn't really know what was going on and school didn't open up and that was it. I really didn't understand education at the time, but I understand it now, because education is very important to each and everybody. At one time education meant more to us to get a job, right now, we can't get a job right now because we don't have the education, some people today didn't get a chance to finish the school thing and half of them can't read and write and that's bad on the black people, its real bad. I got mine, I had to go to New York to get mine, so I went to Chester New York in '59, stayed there until '64, '65 and went to school up there. I still didn't finish school because something happened, I got married and everything, I just moved on from there. I came back to school when school reopened and they put me in the 8th grade according to what I had learned, the little test they give you, and then I went to the 11th grade and dropped out to take care of my family and that was it.

I retired from the military in 92. 1971-1976. I went into inactive army until 1992, in the meantime, I had a full-time job working at the prison for 25 years and retired from that and I got my GED in the military and now I work a part time job at this place called Jemini. If school had not closed, I really would have loved to teach kids things, but as long as I have my health, I am good. The closing of the school hurt me and a lot of people because a lot of other people were going to school and we couldn't go. Kids today, don't drop out of school, go to school. Thank GOD for everything, I'm an old man now and I am glad, because our Father took care of me all these years and I thank GOD for it.

Mattie Paige -Wiley

 I was in the 7th grade. I went to the high school for one year and the next year the school closed. I found out about the school closing because a neighbor of ours Mrs. Annie Mae Griggs came to talk to my mother and told her that you know that the schools are not going to open and you got to do something with those children of yours. With her working with my mom, they were able to somehow get with the American Friends Services Committee. and they sent me to Philadelphia to go to school and once we were there because they came up with some rule that the children had to be adopted in order to stay. So, we were immediately sent to Dayton, Ohio. When I heard that school was closed, at first I was happy, oh gee wheeze, we don't have to go to school but I guess when reality set in and we found out that they were not going to open in just a couple of weeks or something, this was going to be a long term something, it was more what am I going to do with myself, how we gonna learn, so I guess that when some of the sadness set in, it was some other sadness because of the fear that by then we had learned that we were not going to be at home and being away and not be able to be with your parents and all of that was fearful.

I was at Dayton, Ohio for two years and came back home and I ended up going to New York attending school there. I never did go back to school here when school reopened, I was in the 10th grade because after that I went back, and stopped and went to night school and completed. And I got married, and then I felt that I needed to continue my education so I went back to night school. I didn't finish that until 1983.

At the end of the school closing, households of 20, and 21 children missed the entire 5 years. They will tell how this affected them and their siblings.

Nathaniel Eanes

When school closed, I was 16. I found out that school had closed because I couldn't go to school. I heard it through the radio and I heard that John F. Kennedy announced that Free School would be open on a certain day. School closed in 1959 and reopened in '63. That's how I really found out. I had in my family 21 brothers and sisters. When school was closed, did any of you that was school aged go to school? "When school was closed, no we didn't go to school anywhere.

When school closed, I stayed around on the farm, raised

tobacco, cutting wood, working for my dad. When I heard that school would be open, I jumped for joy. I was glad that schools reopened, I went back to school. I did my best. I stayed until I graduated from R. R. Moton High School.

I would like to say- well when they closed the school, it kinda hurt me to see that school was closed. Something else that hurt me too, during those years they closed the school. My mother and father had to pay taxes for us, we didn't get any benefit from the tax money because they closed the schools and we still had to pay the taxes. And even until today when I go down town to do my personal and property tax, I tell that lady down there, give me a break, my father paid taxes for five years, we didn't get any benefit of it. Give ...me a break. Sometime I tell people that since I missed those years of education, paid the taxes, give my grandchildren a chance to get a college degree free. Give them a college degree for the mistake that was made, I feel they deserve a pass to a college degree free.

Now I am retired from the Virginia Highway Department, which is known now as VDOT and I retired there with 30 years of service. I stay around the house, do what I have to do around home. I am looking for a part time job at the moment, but its kind of hard to find. So, I stay around home, doing the chores and keep it up, cut the grass, see that I got firewood to keep the home more comfortable for us to live in during the winter

Malvin Eanes

I was 7 years old when school closed. I found out about the school closing when my parents were talking about it and they said the school will be closing. I didn't think too much of it at the time.

When I heard about it, I was very saddened, very disappointed. I felt like it was just a month or two type things, I didn't realize it was going to be as long as it was.

My father owned a farm, so when school closed, we had to work on the family farm. I wasn't able to go to school anywhere because it was too many siblings at the time to go to another school or go anyplace else. My mother taught us the best that she could, and my older siblings kind of helped us younger ones to read and write to the best of their ability.

When school reopened four years later, I was very excited to go back; a little nervous and a little scary. I was most certainly glad to be back in school. I graduated from Prince Edward County Public High School in 1973, at the age of 21, married with a child, and a full-time night job.

What would I have like to have been or done if school had not closed? That's a good question. I always wanted to play sports, so I wanted to continue to go to school and possibly go to college and maybe play sports.

I retired two years ago from Longwood University after 34 years as the Recreation Supervisor. I just hope that something like the school closing never happens again. It really did affect a lot of the people in Prince Edward County, but through the grace of God, He gave us strength to overcome.

Vincent Eanes

When school closed, I was in the 2nd grade promoted to the 3rd. The teacher told us about schools closing a few months before school closed. We were too young, we didn't understand. I was kinda glad, it was exciting, because I really didn't like school at that time. Really at that time I was kind of glad. I was happy, I was young, I didn't want to go to school. I didn't' know what I was in for. Then I felt sorry because I was in the tobacco field, when I could be in school, I wished I was in school. We didn't go anywhere, wasn't able to go anywhere, just stayed home, milk cows, chop wood, and slop hogs, that type of thing. Our parents raised us and taught us how to be respectful. They kept us in line and did the usual thing and day by day, that is how we lived. At my home the only thing that talked about school was the radio, we didn't talk about it in the house as a family. The subject hardly ever come up.

When it reopened, then I guess 6 months when it kinda got close that it would be open, that it was a strong possibility that school would open, then I was a little older and I was excited and looking forward to going back to school. I was glad when it opened. I just fell along with the shift. Still not knowing how things were going to turn out, so I just go along with the shift and I was glad when it did open up.

When school opened, they had lost all paperwork, no paper trail; being I didn't go anywhere they gave us a test. If you were a certain age you would go to different parts of the school, I had to go to the gym and they gave us this test. They had a certain way they would test you. They judged us by our test scores. My test scores were so low, I had to go back to grade school next to kindergarten and start all over again. It really wasn't no particular grades when it opened up. It took a couple years to find out where we were.

I had 21 siblings, 7 sisters and 14 brothers. It really was 25 siblings; I was 50 years old when I found out that. Most all of them were affected, my mother had 3 previous miscarriages. Most all of them was school age when school closed. When school reopened 15 of my sisters and brothers went back, one didn't go back, and 2 didn't graduate. I graduated when I was 24 years old, got married of course, and went on to further my education. I am the only one that went to college. I went to seminary school and got 8 years of college and got a Bachelor Degree in Religion Education, and that is going well. I am excited about that. God is able.

If school had not closed, (pause) (voice breaking with pain) it hurt, because if mom could have sent me away, I would have been like other kids, I could have gotten my basis, whether I would have used it or not, I wanted that chance, because I don't have what I ought to have (tearful). If mom and dad could have sent me away, (pause) now I need my basis. I would have had the chance whether I could have accomplished it, long gone, long gone. This is one of the most devastating things ever happen to any individual and I don't want any other children to fall in the trap that Prince Edward has fallen into. I want it to be known, what happened and no shame to this game, but I want the story to get out and be told. As of now, I am a full-time pastor and very excited and it is going well.

Therman Otis Banks

 In 1959, I was in the fifth grade. I found out about the school closing by people talking and my parents. I was upset and wondering if I was going to get an education or not. When school closed, I stayed out, I didn't go to school anywhere else. When Free School reopened in Prince Edward County, Farmville, I went back to the elementary school at

Branch 2 to the 5th grade. When I went back, I was of age so they skipped me, I went to the grade they put me in. I missed two grades. When I went back, I was old, they put me in the 10th grade. I finished high school in 1973. My mother had 20 children all together. At that time, I had 10 brothers and eight sisters when school was closed. At least 2 or 3 of my sisters and brothers went away to school and the rest of us stayed at home the five years our public schools were closed.

If school had not closed, I would like to been a supervisor. I like to supervise people, I did want to go to college, but I never had the opportunity because while school being closed, I got married early and I didn't get a chance to finish my education, and I was married with a family, and having a family I just couldn't go back and finish my education like I wanted to because I had obligations and responsibilities as a husband and a father, and I didn't get a chance to finish my education.

Well, I was just hoping that people could, even if you were of age could go back and maybe I was hoping that they could maybe give us some kind of grant so people can go back some kind of way to get their education, finish or pursue their education even though they are of age, because I think education is valuable and I think that if anyone wants to go back and pursue their education, I think there should be some kind of grant for them to do so.

I am retired from the Department of Corrections and now I drive the school bus for Prince Edward County.

(I informed him after our interview of the Brown Scholarship in which anyone directly affected could go back to school tuition free).

In 1964-1965 the Prince Edward County Public Schools reopened and for the first time in five years children were enrolled in regular Public School.

Edward Morton

 When school closed, I attended Mercy Seat School in Hampden Sydney and I was in the 4th grade. I found out about the schools being closed, friends told me and I really thought it was just a joke; it wasn't going to be closed very long. Well the first couple years we were kind of excited about it because we stayed at home and that was pretty good, but after it went on and on, we realized that (he chuckled) that something was a problem going on there.

Well when school closed, I didn't do basically anything really for about three years, then I went to Philadelphia and went to school. When school reopened, then I came back. I didn't go to Free school, but I did come back to Robert R. Moton to finish up and graduated in 1970.

I feel like if school had not closed it, it really made me grow up fast. It made me grow up real fast and when it closed, I was upset because I really didn't understand what was going on, but with the grace of God, I did get a chance to finish school and the high school and I went on, was a very successful young man working in the Richmond Public Schools where I retired working with Special Ed. Kids. I am substitute teaching in Richmond called the Real School.

If school had not closed, I think I could have been many things I wanted to be, but I really felt it helped me as a young man to grow up, to know that this happened to me and I was bitter, but, it ended up I was a successful young man. You know, did well with myself.

Well, I think people should know more about it and it should be taught to our young generation coming up and they should know that it was a struggle in Prince Edward County and that this happened to young black men and women. I called it the dark ages. The lost ages for us really, I call it.

Gwendolyn Wise-Love

 I was in the 3rd grade when school closed in 1959. I went to New York to live with two aunts and went to school at PS 186 Elementary School. I was 11 years old going to the 5th grade. I came back here and went to school one year in 1963, which was my last year here in Prince Edward County. I left in 1964, went to New York, and came back to Prince Edward County Schools to finish at the Robert R. Moton High School. I have 2 daughters.

Elizabeth Spradley

I was in the 3rd grade when school closed. I found out from my mother and friends. When I heard that school was

 closed, I was surprised, amazed, terrified, it was just ugly seeing the locks on the doors, it's like once upon a time, they said you couldn't lock church doors, and I felt that they had locked the church door up on me. It hurt me, a lot of my friends left me and went away, we had to leave home staying with our sister, leaving our mother to work, still taking my parents tax

dollars, we are not in school, I just think it was terrible. During school closing I went with my sisters for two years, who lived in Jetersville, Virginia and I went there, I went to the 4th grade at Central Elementary School in Charlotte Court House, Virginia I think the 5th grade, I was in Jetersville school in Amelia, and each year I was with my sisters and half of a year, I was with a friend of my mother's and daddy's in Charlotte Court House, Mr. Wilbert Pew and Pattie Spencer Pew. I was still in Virginia, wherever I went, I was in Amelia County a year, Charlotte County a second year, My first year we went to the tar shacks up here where Moton Museum is now, Edwilda Allen taught there, we had activities there. I remembered her because she was such a sweet person. Then after that we went to the basement of the church of First Baptist, Reverend Goodman Douglas.

When school reopened, we had the Free School in 63, at that time they had the 7th grade and my 7trh grade teacher came out of New York, I forgot what part of New York she came from, but her last name was Ms. Penna, P-e-n-n-a and me and several of my friends were in her homeroom. She was a very nice person, but when school opened up during that time Mr. Cooley, from Charlotte County was our Principal and he was a great guy. The year of '64, I skipped the 5th grade and went to the 7th grade and Ms. Penna was my teacher and at that time 7th grade was at the high school, Robert Russell Moton.

Now, I am retired. If school had not closed, the two things that I wanted to be was a school teacher and a nurse. I ended up being a Nurse's Aide for 30 years and I enjoyed it, I worked with elderly people. I would like to say the main thing the school closing was a very hurting time for me, but I am trying to overcome it. I am doing pretty good, but a lot of my friends are deceased. We didn't have enough time together because the school was closed and you know I just blame everything on that time, because we lost a lot. I would have liked to have finished my education, but I went in a different direction, I could have finished school. I completed the 9th grade, I would have graduated in 1967, if I had stayed in school. The school closing was one of the most terrible things that the school board could have done.

Laneuville Scott Walker

When school closed, I had completed the 6th grade and passed to the 7th grade. I found out about the school closing; my mother told me. When you heard that school had closed, I really couldn't believe it. We had always had schools to attend, so it just didn't seem real.

After school closed, the first year, I attended a make-shift school in the basement of my church, St. James A.M.E. Church in Prospect, VA. I continued to read and study books I had at home. The next year, I went to live with a family friend, Miss Hattie Jones, who lived in Appomattox County. She said I could come and live with her and attend school free of charge. The only thing she wanted me to do was the cooking and cleaning. At this time, I was 12 years old, and had never done much cooking, but I had watched my mother, who was a very good cook. I had done a lot of cleaning, so that was not a problem. The next two years I lived with one of my best friend's aunt and uncle, Mr. and Mrs. Ross Edwards, in Appomattox County. Mr. and Mrs. Edwards also took in one of my friends who lived across the road from me in Prospect. This friend and I shared a room. They also took in a family, which consisted of the mother, father, and 5 children.

My father died on March 26, 1960. My mother continued to live in Prospect and work as a domestic worker. When schools reopened, I returned home to Prospect and resumed my education at Robert R. Moton High School, as a 10th grader. I graduated in June 1966, as Class Valedictorian.

I am currently working for the State of Virginia University. I worked in the insurance industry, in several positions including Corporate Secretary and Assistant Vice President.as a Case Consultant, prior to this job, after graduating from Virginia Commonwealth.

If school had not closed, since I was blessed to have only missed one year of school due to the closing, I would have pursued my education as I did, but would not have had to leave home to do it. The school closing caused my family to be separated much too soon. I had never lived away from my mother, brother and extended family members until I had to leave to attend school. The families I lived with were really nice people, who showed so much compassion at a time when it was needed. They opened their homes and welcomed me and others with loving care. But still, there was the void of missing my family. When my brother went up north to attend school and I went to Appomattox, I had no idea that we would never live together as a family again. That really hurt. But even at my young age then, I realized that I was one of the lucky ones, who had the opportunity to attend school, while so many others in Prince Edward were deprived of that opportunity.

Ida Mae Reed-Walton

When school closed, I had just completed the second grade and passing to the third grade.

I found out about the school closing from my Mother and Father. At first, I was happy because the trip to school was cold. The school bus was cold and if my family missed the bus, we had to walk to school in cold weather. I became sad when I found out that we could not go to school at all.

The first-year school was closed; five of us did not attend school anywhere. The next two years we went to a training center at the St. Matthew Lutheran Church which is the church our mother grew up in. The following year we went to Lunenburg County Public Schools. The year after that the free schools opened and we returned to Prince Edward. My parents were busy trying to find a school system for us to attend so we wouldn't be idle around the house.

When school re-opened, I rejoiced because I could go back home instead of living part time in Lunenburg County. I had just passed to the 6th grade but after a month, I was moved to the 7th grade.

Currently I am retired and working part time providing assistance to an individual with a disability. After graduation in 1969, I attended Baltimore Regional First Aid & Nursing Assistance Program. I worked at St. Agnes Catholic Hospital and attended their Nursing Assistance Program also. A year later, I married my husband, Joseph Walton, and moved back home to Virginia to start a family. In addition to raising my family, I have had a variety of jobs to include babysitting, caring for the elderly and working in textile and garment factories. I would like to have been a nurse or a cosmetologist.

Danny Morton

 I was in the 2nd grade when school closed at Mercy Seat School in Hampden Sydney. I found out the day of school opening that school was closed when I went up to the school and three white men was there saying that there will be no school today. I was thinking that it was just for that day, not for five years. We went back home and my grandmother said that school was closed and there will be no school this year, that there wasn't any funding for the school so I found out from my grandmother, tell you the truth.

When I heard that school was closed, being at a young age of 7, I was really happy that school was closed, because it was something that kids go through, not knowing that it was going to be closed for five years and affect my life like that. After I realized that school was going to be closed, we didn't actually know how long it was going to be closed. We had to go through home schools because we had teachers there, which really weren't teachers, they were there to try to help us read and write and teach math at the Society Hall.

My grandmother, Victoria Brown was a school teacher and she got a job at Appomattox County. My mother sent me with her and we went to Carver Price for four years. I started out in the 2nd grade up there and when they reopened the Free School in '63 in Prince Edward County, I was in the 6th grade because I missed one year. We commuted every day and I started back at Worsham Middle school in Prince Edward. I finished school at Prince Edward County High School which was RR Moton when I started back, but they changed it to Prince Edward County

High School before I graduated. We kicked that, not knowing the school was named by the county. Instead of explaining that, they just said they were going to do it. That is another reason we were upset, because they changed the school that was named after a Black man.

Now, I am working for the State of Virginia with the Department of Correction of Education as a teacher of the Powhatan Correctional Center and I have been doing that for 25 years. I think if the school hadn't closed, I don't think I would have gone into the masonry, I think I would have stayed in college and finished school and maybe have been a school teacher, even though I teach now, but I teach in a vocational field instead in an educational field.

I went to school at Virginia State for two years. Knowing what I know now about what went on back in the time school was closed, and why they were closed, and who closed the schools. I had friends of mine who told me that the Board of Supervisors were the ones who closed the schools. They were the ones who did not match the government's funding. At that time, they were already building the Prince Edward Academy, which we didn't know anything about what they were doing. They had already planned to close the schools before they closed it. As soon as they got Prince Edward Academy built, they closed the schools. The plan was in effect all the time.

By not having Blacks on the Board of Supervisors, we were left in the dark; we didn't know what was going on, so now we have Blacks on the Board of Supervisors, and getting some insight on some of the stuff going on in the county. I still think overall I had a good life; it wasn't a hard one, I still accomplished a lot of stuff, but I was one of the lucky ones for not having to be out of school for five years. Like I said my grandmother was a teacher and we stayed out of school for one year going from house to house and to the

Society School. But as a whole, I think I still benefited a lot in life and accomplished a lot of things.

Catherine Hines-Smith

 I was in the first grade when school closed. I found out about the school closing when my mother just said it closed up, schools had closed. When I heard about it, it wasn't really a reaction at the time, it didn't hit me until later in life. When school closed the first two years I stayed at home on the farm.

My mother only had a second-grade education, so we just didn't function on much education in the family. My mother was well read in Bible things like that, so she taught me what she knew. Her thing was always, honey get an education and get a good job. I went to Martinsville and they tested me and I started in the 3rd grade. Before school was reopen, I want to say, I spent that whole year from my mother. I cried at night, that lady couldn't comfort me like my mother could, she was an old lady, she was wealthy, she was black, but it was just a different setup for me, leaving being poor to go and live with somebody being rich, learning all she wanted me to learn and not having my mother at all and me and my mother was so close.

I remember dropping a little card, you know the card you get in a greeting card? Putting that in the mail and telling my mother come and get me (laughed), my mother said she never got that card, I guess it got stuck in the mail. Good thing, because she probably would have come and got me, but I couldn't come home, not even for the holidays, and a lot of nights I went home, you know we walked to school and I would just cry, I want my ma. And the girls down the street, I always remember, she was like me poor, not from my area. Like I say, this lady was richer, in the community the houses got cheaper and this girl became my friend and she was on my level, looked like. More than the upper-class people in that area. She would walk with me to school and she and I would talk a lot during that time and made me feel a little more comfortable.

But the lady was wonderful, she took care of me, did everything for me, brought my clothes, my own private room and bath, she was as sweet as could be, but she just couldn't take the place of my mother, but I did get education for that year and then that is when school opened back that summer I came on back home and I went to Prince Edward. When Free School reopened, I started off at Worsham, so that was another testing process. Then I went to the fourth grade and spent the rest of the time at Worsham and then moved on to R. R. Moton, when they had the big debate about changing the name, I was involved in that. I kept going and as a matter of, I would have been 22 when I came out of school, but thank God for Mr. Penn.

A friend of mine had a friend that took a class and we went and talked to Mr. Penn about if we could find something that offered us Math and English for the summer for credit, he would let us go ahead to the next grade if we passed. So I was supposed to be going to the 11th grade, so that summer I leave home again and I go to Suffix, Virginia and take math and I believe it was a science course, that they offered as if you were going for the whole year, and I came back and went to the 12th grade instead of the eleventh grade. And that's how I graduated at 21 in 1972 instead at 22. It was three of us girls, and we were trying to get out of school so bad and Mr. Penn, we figured out a way and he went along with us with that. He said if yall can find a school that is offering those courses as a year course, then I would do that for you all and he did. Me and three girlfriends went and stayed with strangers that year. Packed up and left for the summer, it was worth it and we came back and we went into the twelfth grade. I had to take double English, a lot of double courses to make it my grade level at what I needed to get out of school, because I graduated with my little degrees and honors. I graduated from Prince Edward County High School, that is the year they changed the name from R. R. Moton High School.

Right now, I have my own business and my daughter has a business, so I work part time for her and then I work my own business. I am the owner of Catherine's Waterside Adult Care. I take care of senior patients. I used to work the factories, got out of the factories work, started as an aide and loved nursing and went on to college and got my nursing degree and between loving it and the financial need, I decided to do my own business. I saw what the community needed, that people needed housing, people didn't need to go into nursing homes right away and those were the clients I started targeting.

If school had not closed, that meant I would have been coming out of school at 18, 19. I could have gone on to college, maybe got my master degree or my doctorate. I found out when I was going to school, it was more of an issue of getting us out of school and in five years, you get broken English, that I hadn't learned, broken grammar, not knowing how to spell and so all that carried over in my life as I went to college. I had to go and take those classes to make up for that when I started off. When I went to nursing school, I had to carry my little pocket dictionary, when didn't have those little computers then where you could just tap in and find out how to spell a word. I had to carry that little paper dictionary that whole time I was in nursing school when I had to write my medical notes, I would be looking at the dictionary making sure I knew how to spell my words or my homework time, it took me longer, because I had poor grammar and the reading I hadn't gotten and I should have gotten when I was in elementary school, because by that time they were trying to get us out of school, even when school opened. We had a few good teachers that really worked with us, that was so much to learn to make up for five years and you are older than you are supposed to be and you trying to get out, the teachers did the best they could, it was just so…you couldn't do.

I hear people say, get over it, forgive. God teaches me to forgive for it, but I still can't get over it because that effected my life, even now and, even sometimes like I say writing my notes, my spelling still bad or going back to school, I remember having such a hard time in chemistry because I didn't get it all when I was in school and at my age who got time to tutor me now. I wish I could have, I think if I could do anything now is to have someone tutor me to learn how to spell all the right words, or pronouncing the words the correct way, being able to just read any book I wanted to without stumbling through it, trying to figure out the pronunciation of it. That's what I would want to do.

Aldrena Pryor-Thirkill

When school closed I was somewhere between 12 or 13. I found out really by word of mouth, I think the teachers kind of mentioned to us the last day of school before they closed that summer of 1959, that the schools wouldn't be open the next year. Then the next year came around and we discovered that the schools were not going to open. So, during that first year we really didn't go to school at all. Just kind of worked on the farm, visited my sister in New

York. I don't quite remember, but I may have visited my dad because he lived in Baltimore.

When I heard that school had closed, I felt really- just kind of numb. That was the main source of our social entertainment for children back in those days, you know, didn't really get to be around a lot of other children except for being in school. They were like far away; we had a couple that was close and we would play with them, but other than that, it was kind of a numb feeling, knowing that you couldn't go to school. We did try to go with a few other families, I think our families tried, they rented a house when they thought it was in Appomattox County, but then after I think a few days, maybe a week or so going there, someone discovered that the house was actually in Prince Edward County, so they told us we could not attend school in Appomattox because we didn't live there. (Laughing) so we had, you know, I think that was the first year. Then after that my mom sacrificed to send us to Baltimore, Maryland to live with one of her brothers and his wife. One of her sisters also went along with us and her grandson.

The culture shock was leaving this area, which of course obvious country, and going to a major city like Baltimore where you went like from dirt and sand to sidewalks and many cars, so that was quite an adjustment. And I guess feelings run small and wide. I don't remember much, initially you felt like am I good enough to be associated with others, why are they closed? Why did they pick on me, you know, what did I do, you know, kind of like self-blaming, and then like even your family would say like, don't talk about that, you know, just don't mention it, but they didn't tell why you shouldn't. I don't- like it was somewhat like an embarrassment? But then later on I started to learn things and realized that was really unjust and it wasn't right, then the feelings changed like we need to do something about it because this is not the way we should be treated. You know like everybody deserves an education, so why shouldn't we have the same privilege that everybody else. So that's kind of at first, I think at first it's like lack of knowledge, you don't know, so you just go along with the way things have always been, and then later on the feelings change like this shouldn't be this way, you know this shouldn't happen and doing this type of treatment, so that is what I mean when I say that it goes from maybe insignificant at the time, but in time, it does become very significant, you know, that we should be allowed an education.

When school reopened, we returned back here to Prince Edward County and went to the first year the free schools opened. We stayed three years in all. We would come back during the summer and if we get transportation sometimes during the holidays. And we stayed in Baltimore and returned there.

Sherry Jeannette Brown

 I believe I was nine going on ten when school closed. We didn't find out about the school closing until we were scheduled to go back that fall. My mother did not share with me of the school closing; I think it was unbeknown to her too. When I heard that school was closed, I couldn't believe it, that a school could close down and deny us from going, because you look forward to going back to school in the fall when the summer is over, we are going back to school, so my mother shared with me that we wouldn't be going, I was surprised.

261

My mother kept me out of school the first year thinking it was going to reopen, because they were saying that it would open, so she said ok, we will wait. Then the second year they said it would open, so we waited. The third year, she didn't trust them; she said you are going to Albemarle County to live with your father. So, I left in that third year and went to Albemarle County.

When school reopened, my mother allowed me to stay in Albemarle because she wasn't sure how long the Free School would remain open, so she didn't send me back until 1966, when she was sure the schools would remain open. I was in the 6th grade when I came back, because the two years I missed I should have been in the 8th grade, so at the end of 6th grade she brought me back and I finished school here. When I came back my Mom was living in Cumberland County, so I went to Cumberland County for one semester and then we moved back to Farmville, and I finished out in Farmville in 1970.

It came up in 1969, it was R. R. Moton, that year my graduation, they came to us and they said in order for the schools to integrate, we would have to change the school name because white people do not want to go to a school, they call it with a (colored person's) name. So that year, my graduation year, that is when the school changed its name, so I graduated under Prince Edward County High School. And I even had a hard time remembering the name of the school because you are so sure that you was going to graduate under R. R. Moton and someone was just saying recently that the older generation still say R. R. Moton not caring to say Prince Edward County High School, even though they graduated from Prince Edward High School, they say I graduated from Moton.

At first, I did factory work when I got out of school, then Prudential Insurance, they were paying more, I worked for

Wheaten Glass then I went into the school system in 1979, the latter part of the year I started working for Vinton Public School System in New Jersey. I stayed there until I retired as the library clerk. I became ill so I left New Jersey and I came here and I started working for Cumberland County as a substitute teacher in 2002 and then I switched to Prince Edward working as a substitute in 2010, and I am still working at Prince Edward High School. You always feel an alliance with your Alma Malta.

What I feel is from my point of view, when people closed the schools they did not realize, they did not care about the impact that it would have on the African American families. Because so many of us, our parents depended on us to babysit, so we were older, they went to work, we didn't have latch key kids back then, the schools did not provide afterschool day care, but they knew if they had an older child in the home, that when the older child came home, they could take care of the younger child, so they took away the latchkey child from the parent.

Another problem, some children never went to school anywhere. They stayed out of school for many years. I went away, but you lose that bond that you had with your parents, because now you come home after so many years, like I stayed on for five years, I came home, I had to learn my mom all over again, because I didn't grow up with her. I left as a young child of 11 and when I came back, I was a teenager, I was 16, so thank God I had people who raised me correctly, but those are your formative years. Your tween years, your adolescence years, when you need a parent, but you know, God kept me, but a lot of young people, they ran the streets and I think that is the problem in Farmville of the high poverty rate, that's the reason, when you take away education, people don't value education now, because they were never taught to value it, so I feel that they didn't care whether they did a disservice or not, they thought we were animals, so they treated us like animals, so they treated us like a dog, a cow, a cat and send this animal off, like any animal you separate an animal from its parents and you take this animal, so they did not care, our parents loved us as much as they loved their children just because we were African Americans didn't mean that our parents didn't have that love for us as a parent would have for a child.

My mother suffered with me being gone, because she had to give up her child to go live somewhere else and couldn't see her child grow up. I was the only one in school because my brother and I are eight years apart, so she only had to part with me, so when you think of that, I was her only child at that time so she had sent her only child, and a girl to live with someone else. Although it was my father, my parents had a tumultuous relationship, so for her to send me to live with him was a very great sacrifice for her, all because someone felt that it wasn't important for Blacks to go to school.   It is hurtful, but by God's grace, I got over it.

Fifty years later, regrets for that era has1 been documented for the historical closing of Prince Edward County Public Schools. The regrets are as follows, The Commonwealth of Virginia with the House Joint Resolution No. 613, January 30, 2003, a plaque was erected on the courthouse grounds in the town of Farmville, Virginia which displayed a Profound Regret and a Light of Resolution from the current Prince Edward Board of Supervisors in 2008.

Moments in History

REGRETS

HOUSE JOINT RESOLUTION NO. 613

Attachment A to Info Memo No. 105 Page 1 of 2 HOUSE JOINT RESOLUTION NO. 613 Expressing the General Assembly's profound regret over the 1959-1964 closing of the public schools in Prince Edward County, Virginia. Agreed to by the House of Delegates, January 30, 2003 Agreed to by the Senate, February 13, 2003 WHEREAS, the Commonwealth's constitutional commitment to "establish and maintain an efficient system of public free schools," as articulated in the 1902 Constitution of Virginia, produced mixed interpretations following the 1954 United States Supreme Court decision in Brown v. Board of Education declaring segregation in public schools "inherently unequal," and was construed in Virginia to support massive resistance; and WHEREAS, in 1956 the Constitution of Virginia was amended to authorize the General Assembly and local governing bodies to appropriate funds to assist students to go to public or to nonsectarian private schools, and the General Assembly "enacted legislation to close any public schools where white and colored children were enrolled together, to cut off state funds to such schools, to pay tuition grants to children in nonsectarian private schools, and to extend state retirement benefits to teachers in newly created private schools"; and WHEREAS, in 1959 local officials closed the public school system of Prince Edward County in defiance of the school desegregation order in the Brown decision, an act constituting a unique event in American history; and WHEREAS, for a period of five years, the public schools in Prince Edward County remained closed to more than 2,300 African-American children, who, with only a few exceptions, remained unschooled for at least four of these five years; and WHEREAS, the founding of "free schools" to educate African-American children in the 1963- 1964 school year provided the African-American students of Prince Edward County with opportunities for formal education for the first time since the 1959 closing of the Prince Edward County Public Schools; and WHEREAS, as part of this massive resistance movement in Virginia, Prince Edward County cut off tax money earmarked for public schools, and a private academy was immediately established and supported by those same tax dollars, in effect creating vouchers and local tuition grants exclusively for white children in Prince Edward County; and WHEREAS, while the lengthy battle waged by the National Association for the Advancement of Colored People (NAACP) for equality in separate educational facilities across the South from the late 1930s through the 1940s had produced minimal progress, judicial challenges led by attorney Oliver Hill in Virginia were prodding the Commonwealth toward equality within segregation; and Attachment A to Info Memo No. 105 Page 2 of 2 WHEREAS, the 1950 United States Supreme Court ruling in Sweatt v. Painter stated that the creation of a segregated law school at the University of Texas to serve one African-American applicant could not provide the quality education offered at the existing law school, prompting the NAACP to shift its focus from equality in separate facilities to desegregation in public education; and WHEREAS, the African-American community of Prince Edward County was one of five plaintiffs in the landmark Brown case, and the closing of the Prince Edward County Public Schools was the climactic event of a decade-long struggle for educational opportunity by the African-American community in this rural, agricultural region of Southside Virginia; and WHEREAS, not only did African Americans suffer, but citizens throughout Prince Edward County were affected as well by the deep, contentious division created by the denial of public education to the African-American community; and WHEREAS, it must also be remembered that at least 350 white students whose parents were unable to afford private school tuition were also deprived of free public education for five years; and WHEREAS, the closing of the Prince Edward County schools severely affected the education of African-American students, wounding the human spirit and ultimately contributing to job and home losses, family displacements and separations, and a deep sense of despair within the African-American community; and WHEREAS, in 1964, the United States Supreme Court found, in Griffin v. County School Board, that "closing the Prince Edward County schools while public schools in all the other counties of Virginia were being maintained denied the petitioners and the class of Negro students they represent the equal protection of the laws guaranteed by the Fourteenth Amendment" and called for "quick and effective relief" to "put an end to the racial discrimination practiced against these petitioners under authority of the Virginia laws"; and WHEREAS, the Griffin Court acknowledged the constitutional right of these Prince Edward students "to an education equal to that afforded by the public schools in the other parts of Virginia"; now, therefore, be it RESOLVED by the House of Delegates, the Senate concurring, That the General Assembly expresses its profound regret over the 1959-1964 closing of the public schools in Prince Edward County, Virginia; and, be it RESOLVED FURTHER, That the General Assembly urge the citizens of the Commonwealth to celebrate in all appropriate ways the 50th anniversary of the Brown v. Board of Education decision in 2004 by acknowledging the benefits and fairness of equality and becoming familiar with the history of the massive resistance movement, in the belief that a more educated, enlightened, and tolerant population will learn from history and will reject absolutely any such discriminatory practices in the future.

NOW THEREFORE BE IT RESOLVED

That we, the undersigned members of the Prince Edward County Board of Supervisors, believe that the closing of public schools in our county from 1959 to 1964 was wrong: and we grieve for the way lives were forever changed, for the pain that was caused, and for how those locked doors shuttered the opportunities and barricaded the dreams our children had for their own lifetimes: and for all wounds known and unknown: we regret those past actions. Signed by the current Prince Edward County Board of Supervisors. On the front of the regret is The Light of Reconciliation.

The Light of Reconciliation

The Light of Reconciliation Illuminated in the Courthouse Bell Tower on July 21, 2008, by the Board of Supervisors of Prince Edward County, in honor of Barbara Rose Johns and the students of Robert Russa Moton High School, and all the children of our county for their historic role in ending public school segregation in the United States, and with sorrow for closing schools. When we raise our eyes to see this light, may we also incline our hearts and minds to shine our own light of reconciliation toward all people.

The Civil Rights Memorial Completed

The Civil Rights Memorial was completed and displayed on Capitol Square July 21, 2008 in observance of a huge gathering of media, an estimated 4,000 people in attendance as the monument was unveiled. Among those that participated in the unveiling were Former Governor Tim Kaine, Leslie Griffin, son of one of the figures depicted, Reverend L. Francis Griffin, John Stokes, a student of the 1951 walkout, Nikki Giovonni, Blair Underwood and Rita Odom Moseley.

Letters

First Lady, Lisa Collis

Dear Rita – So good to hear from you and congratulations on the book. I hope it is going well.

I understand that you want a statement on the impetus for the Civil Rights Memorial at the Capitol. Here is how my part was started.

We had been living in the Executive Mansion for several months when our youngest daughter, Eliza (8 years old), and I started a practice of walking around the Capitol grounds at night with our dog. She liked running up to all the monuments and reading the plaques out loud. One night, she asked me "How come these people have statues"? I told her that these were individuals that people in their time thought had done something important. She then asked me, "Well how come there isn't a statue for Rosa Parks"? I told her that she was right. Rosa Parks was a hero deserving of a statue, but that she wasn't a Virginian so probably wouldn't have a statue here on our Capitol grounds.

The whole conversation got me thinking and I had several conversations with Mark about the memorials on the grounds and why we had never honored Virginia's civil rights heroes. He encouraged me to pursue it and so I started reading more about Virginia's Civil Rights history, discussing the idea with some legislators, most importantly Sen. Henry Marsh, and with Secretary Sandy Bowen, historians and others. To a person, everyone I spoke with about the idea was enthusiastic. A small informal group was organized to discuss the idea, and after a meeting or two a consensus built around the story of the Moton protest as the most compelling subject for a possible memorial.

In early 2005, House Joint Resolution No. 790 established a commission to study and recommend an appropriate memorial in Capitol Square to commemorate the students of Robert R. Moton High School and other persons who contributed to the Civil Rights movement in Virginia.

Hope this is useful, let me know if you need additional information.

Yours truly,

Lisa

After receiving a personal letter from Principal Bash in 2003, explaining his actions of quitting and refusing to continue as principal of the white children's school when they decided to close the Black children's school, we continued our friendship with visits, phone calls and letters until his passing.

Excerpts from letters of Dr. James Bash and my response.

25 June 2003

Perhaps a glimpse of my involvement during that historic time may perhaps help you to understand why I am so very pleased to know your efforts have brought a sense of closure to people who were unjustly denied education in Prince Edward County because of an exclusionary decision, the effect of which closed your public school which was funded under the Civil Rights Act of 1964.

On 7 June 1955 a meeting was held in Jarman Auditorium, Longwood College, to rally the population to endorse the closing of Prince Edward Schools rather than abide by decisions ordering desegregation (Brown I – 1954 and Brown II –1955). To my knowledge few, if any, black people were in attendance. As principal of the Farmville High School at that time, I spoke to this gathering in an effort to dissuade those assembled from taking action to close their public schools in defiance of the law of the land as ruled by the United States Supreme Court. I further indicated that I could not, in good conscience, serve as part of a private educational system designed for white children only. My words failed to convince those present at the meeting.

Following this meeting, I submitted my resignation to Mr. Thomas McIllwaine, Superintendent of Schools.

Events during the ensuing years have demonstrated the

wisdom of the desegregation laws, and all who opposed "massive resistance" have since been vindicated. The idea to hold a ceremony for the purpose of awarding honorary diplomas to those now-grown "children is testimony to the truth that progress continues.

I want to offer through you my heartfelt congratulations to the heroes in the struggle for human rights and who received their diplomas thereby alleviating the effects of a painful miscarriage of justice.

I wish you satisfaction as you continue your work with the students and faculty at Prince Edward County High School.

Kudos and plaudits to all who deservedly, wore "cap and gown" on 15 June 2003!

July 8, 2003 - July 15, 2003

Excerpts from my letter in response to James Bash's letter. It took me a week to answer his letter.

Of all the calls and correspondence, I've received since the beginning of the organizing of the Honorary Diploma Program, your letter brought tears to my eyes. Until I received your letter, I never knew or believed there was anyone in your community that even cared or objected to the closing of our schools. Never would I have guessed; it would have been the principal of that school himself.

I am so glad you lived to tell me about this because I will tell it to others. I talk to a lot of people, and believe me, they will be as shocked as I was to find out that you stood up for what you believed in no matter what.

Rita Moseley

November 20, 2003

I am sorry to have waited so long in answering your letter of July 15th, which is very much appreciated"

Your fine letter evoked an emotional response in me not unlike your own reaction to my first letter to you. I am filled with a sense of awe and satisfaction that you, with the help of your parents, found a way to complete your public school education despite the barriers that were stacked against you! It is moreover a tribute to your character that you never "felt anger, bitterness and hatred" over the closing of the public schools in Prince Edward County. The fact that you were able to shelter your own children from such feelings, considering the circumstances of your own childhood, is an outstanding parental accomplishment.

James H. Bash, Ed. D.
Professor Emeritus
University of Virginia

Excerpts from Ken Woodley's letter to me on his contribution to racial healing, Author, The Road to Healing.

July 29, 2015

I had never heard of Massive Resistance when I came to work at The Farmville Herald in 1979 and had no idea The Farmville Herald had fought to close schools rather to integrate them. It shocked me when I was unexpectedly named editor of the Herald in 1990, I could feel God's plan for my life. The editorial page became my pulpit and I preached. Because the editorial pages of the Herald had been a loud voice for Massive Resistance in the 1950's and 1960's, I dedicated my professional life into turning the paper to a loud voice of racial healing and reconciliation. That was why I stayed at the Herald. That was my ministry and the Black community of Prince Edward County who suffered the wound of Massive Resistance was always my particular and beloved congregation, deep in my heart and to the depth of my soul.

Acknowledgements

I am thankful to the following people who assisted me in various capacities in me accomplishing this book. I am forever grateful to Wayne Drumheller, Editor and Founder, The Creative Short Book Writers Project, who made it possible for me to get my first book published and his support for this book.

I want to thank my son, Frank Moseley, II for his continuous support and his invaluable consultation, my daughter JoAnn Moseley-Chambers and my granddaughter, Bryonna Chambers who have always remained supportive.

To all of the interviewees who participated and became the inspiration for me writing this book with over 160 interviews and allowing me to take their pictures wherever I located them.

Dorothy Holcomb, Author, *Educated In Spite of* ... for assisting me in acquiring 13 interviews. Shirley Eanes for her helpful advice in the early stages of my book, Alejia Pride Carrington (Mickie) and Jamie Ruff who has enjoyed watching my success and being extremely helpful in whatever way they could.

My best to Mary Daniel Brown, Kenneth S. Stroupe, Dr. Margaret Blackmon, Ken Woodley, Mary Carroll-Hackett and Heather Lettner-Rust for their tremendous support.

To Betty Jean Ward-Berryman in assisting me with all of my inquires, and my teachers who gave me the foundation to become the person I am today. And always, my dear mother, who understood the significance of an education and took me to live with strangers, Miss Nettie Anderson and Mrs. Laura Anderson, age 81 who died at the age of 107, in assurance that I would obtain an education.

Sources

Interview courtesy of Lester Andrew.

Interview courtesy Senator Henry Marsh.

James Bash piece courtesy of his granddaughter Daisy Rojas.

House Joint Resolution No. 613 courtesy of Viola Baskerville and the late the James Bash.

PECCA courtesy of National Association for the Advancement of Colored People (1960). Emergency Education, Services for Displaced Pupils. Library of Congress, NAACP, Part III: Administrative File, 1909-1969, Box III: A107 (3 folders). Washington, DC: Archived Library of Congress, and Linda Mann, Researcher. (Reverend L. Francis Griffin and Center Map).

http://vacivilrightsmemorial.org/memorial.htm.

https://www.encyclopediavirginia.org/Anderson_Peyton_E_ca_1857-1950 courtesy of Reverend J. Samuel Williams.

History on the wooden built Robert R. Moton High School in Farmville, Virginia and the first commencement exercises in 1931 courtesy of Reverend J. Samuel Williams, Jr.

Number of children deprived of Education courtesy of House Joint Resolution No. 613

Photos and Credits

Book cover photo courtesy of Virginia Department of Historic Resources (DHR).

Photo Civil Rights Memorial completed courtesy of Jeff Saxman and the Civil Rights Memorial Foundation.

Photo taken About the Author courtesy of Cooperative Living Magazine.

Photo enhancement courtesy of Frank Moseley II.

Back cover photo courtesy of Jennifer Overstreet-Wilkerson, Overstreet Photography.

Back cover photo courtesy of Patricia Holcomb's assistance to Author.

Robert Russa Moton (August 26, 1867 – May 31, 1940).

The all-black R. R. Moton High School, located in the town of Farmville in Prince Edward County was named for him.

Transformation of Robert R. Moton High School
(R.R. Moton High School)

Known to a few, an original 'wooden weatherboard' Robert R. Moton School existed in Farmville, Virginia. The Principal of that school was Reverend Peter Price. After the school was torn down the brick two story Robert R. Moton High School was built in the same location. It had only eleven grades. A new Robert R. Moton High School was built across the street from the old one. The 12th grade was added in 1948. The final two story Robert R. Moton High School was built just outside of the Farmville town limits. The previous schools were renamed Mary E. Branch #I (an elementary school)and Mary E. Branch #2 (a middle school), which remained holding the names until the five year closing of the public schools 1959-1964. The Mary E. Branch #2 Middle School building is now the Moton Museum.

PRINCE EDWARD COUNTY and TIMELINE

1896
U.S. Supreme Court landmark decision *Plessy v. Ferguson,* the court found that "separate but equal" was legal in segregation of public facilities.

1902
The Virginia Constitution declares white and colored children shall not be taught in the same school.

1910
Peyton E. Anderson becomes the first African American superintendent of black rural schools in Prince Edward County, a post he will hold until 1915.

1923
Parents of African-American students petition the Prince Edward County School Board to add seventh grade (and later eighth through twelfth) and thus begin creating a high school for black students.

1927
The first Robert R. Moton School opened (now the Prince Edward Recreation Center on South Main St.): first floor houses black elementary students from the town of Farmville, second floor houses black high school students from the whole county.

1931
First Commencement exercises held on June 9, 1931 for thirty 7th graders and June 10, 1931 for eleven seniors at Robert R. Moton High School in Farmville, Virginia. The Principal was Mr. Peter Price.

1939

Robert Russa Moton High School, named for the Virginia-born educator, Robert Russa Moton opens for black students in Prince Edward County. It was one of only twelve black high schools in rural Virginia at that time.

1940's

Enrollment at Moton High School increases to more than 450 by 1950; refusing to erect a new building to handle such overcrowding, in 1948 the county adds three wooden buildings, covered with tar-paper, around the central brick building.

1948

To help with overcrowding in classrooms, tar-paper buildings (referenced as tar papered shacks) were constructed at the all-black Moton High School in Prince Edward County.

1950

Enrollment capacity, Peyton E. Anderson the first African American superintendent of black rural schools in Prince Edward County, dies in Meherrin, Virginia and is buried in the cemetery of Mount Zion Church at the all-black Robert Russa Moton High School in Prince Edward County was only built for 180 students, but it housed 477 students.

1951

Under the leadership of 16 year old Barbara Johns, with her fellow students walked out of their school to protest the horrible conditions of their education as compared to those of the white student's school in the same town. Barbara Johns had visited other schools in other towns and she also saw that they all had nicer schools compared to hers.

Oliver Hill and Spotswood Robinson, lawyers for the National Association for the Advancement of Colored People, arrive in Prince Edward County to help the striking black students of Robert Russa Moton High School.

Virginia NAACP Executive Secretary Lester Banks met with students at Robert Russa Moton School and their parents, telling them that the NAACP is willing to take on their case in an attempt to end segregation. Three days earlier, the students had walked out of school in protest of unequal conditions. After leaving school two weeks earlier in protest of unequal conditions, students at the all-black Robert Russa Moton High School return to class.

The NAACP files the suit *Davis, et al. v. County School Board of Prince Edward County, Virginia* in federal court, challenging the constitutionality of segregated education in Prince Edward County schools on behalf of black students and their parents.
NAACP Attorneys Oliver Hill and Spotswood Robinson was contacted to help Prince Edward County students. The NAACP files the suit Dorothy E. *Davis, et al. v. County School Board of Prince Edward County, Virginia* in federal court. It was one of five cases of the Brown decision.

1952
The U.S. District Court rules against the students of Robert Russa Moton High School in Prince Edward County, upholding the constitutionality of segregated public schools, but orders that the black schools be made physically equal to the white schools.

U.S. Supreme Court hearings begin in the case of *Brown v. Board of Education of Topeka, Kansas*, the five cases from across the country bundled together including the Virginia case of *Davis, et al. v. County School Board of Prince Edward County*.

1953
A new high school was built naming it Robert R. Moton High School for Black Children.

1954

The U.S. Supreme Court rules in *Brown v. Board of Education of Topeka, Kansas*, that segregation in schools is unconstitutional, but fails to explain how quickly and in what manner desegregation is to be achieved. The decision later leads to the Massive Resistance movement in Virginia.

Five cases from Delaware, Kansas, Washington, D.C., South Carolina and Virginia were appealed to the United States Supreme Court when none of the cases was successful in the lower courts. The Supreme Court combined these cases into a single case which eventually became *Brown v. Board of Education*. The five cases were:

Delaware -- Belton v. Gebhart (Bulah v. Gebhart)
Kansas -- Brown v. Board of Education
Washington, D.C. -- Bolling v. Sharp
South Carolina -- Briggs v. Elliot
Virginia – Davis v. County School Board of Prince Edward County

1955

The Supreme Court ruled that the "separate but equal" clause was unconstitutional because it violated the children's 14th amendment rights by separating them solely on the classification of the color of their skin. Chief Justice Warren delivered the court's opinion, stating that "segregated schools are not equal and cannot be made equal, and hence they are deprived of the equal protection of the laws".

The United States Supreme Court announced its decision that "separate educational facilities are inherently unequal." The court's Brown decision overturns the long-standing all deliberate speed" *Plessy* opinion.

Supreme Court issues a ruling known as Brown II outlining that desegregation will occur with "all deliberate speed."

The Gray Commission, a 32 member all white legislative commission appointed by Governor Thomas B. Stanley, who had pledged segregated schools in Virginia, to study the Brown decision, submits its report.

1956

The Stanley Plan created to implement Massive Resistance resulted in the closing of schools in Prince Edward County. Virginia governor Thomas B. Stanley announces a package of massive resistance legislation that will become known as the Stanley Plan. Among other things, the plan gives the governor the power to close any schools facing a federal desegregation order.

U.S. senator Harry F. Byrd calls for a plan of "Massive Resistance" to oppose the integration of public schools in Virginia.

Governor Lindsay Almond Jr. urges the General Assembly to abandon Massive Resistance.

1957

The Fourth Circuit Court of Appeals orders integration of the Prince Edward County Schools "without further delay." But the Prince Edward County School Board wins a stay of this order pending appeal to the U.S. Supreme Court, which turns down the appeal and returns the case to District Judge Sterling Hutcheson to set a precise timetable.

Governor J. Lindsay Almond Jr. closes schools in Charlottesville, Front Royal, and Norfolk, and threatens to close others if they attempt to desegregate.

1959

Both the Virginia Supreme Court of Appeals and the United States District Court overturn the decision of Virginia governor J. Lindsay Almond Jr. to close schools in Front Royal, Charlottesville, and Norfolk.

The U.S. Fourth Circuit Court of Appeals overturns Judge Sterling Hutcheson's ruling in the case of segregated schools in Prince Edward County and orders Prince Edward to integrate its schools by September 1, 1959. NAACP and Prince Edward County lawyers will continue to fight in court over desegregation of the schools for the next five years.

After eight years of court cases and delays related to school desegregation, the Prince Edward County Board of Supervisors votes not to fund public schools in the 1959–1960 school year. Public schools close in Prince Edward County. Prince Edward Academy opens for white students.

1960

The Quaker-oriented American Friends Service Committee begins efforts to send black students denied education in Prince Edward County out of county for their education.

1962

Martin Luther King Jr. visits Prince Edward County.
The U.S. Department of Justice files a friend of the court brief on behalf of the NAACP in their appeal of the closing of the Prince Edward County schools.

1963

U.S. president John F. Kennedy mentions the Prince Edward County school closings in a civil rights address to the U.S. Congress.
U.S. Attorney general Robert F. Kennedy says during a speech: "the only places on earth not to provide free public education are Communist China, North Vietnam, Sarawak, Singapore,

British Honduras—and Prince Edward County, Virginia. Something must be done about Prince Edward County."

The Free Schools Association for Prince Edward County, organized by the administration of U.S. president John F. Kennedy, begins classes. This is the first formal schooling for black students in that county since 1959.

1964

The United Stated Supreme Court rules that Prince Edward Public schools must reopen.

Public Schools in Prince Edward County reopened after closing for five years.

After Prince Edward County's public schools have been closed for the previous five years, the U.S. Supreme Court in *Griffin v. School Board of Prince Edward County* rules that the county has violated the rights of students to an education and orders the Prince Edward County schools to reopen.

About 1,500 students, all but eight were black, attend classes in the Prince Edward County public schools for the first time in five years.

1996

The Martha E. Forrester Council of Women purchased the old Moton High School.

1998

Robert Russa Moton High School is placed on the National Register of Historic Places declared a National Historic Landmark by the U.S. Secretary of Interior, the highest level of historical recognition offered by the federal government. The museum is a reminder of the struggle for Civil Rights in Education and a Center for the Study of Civil Rights in Education.

2001

The Robert Russa Moton Museum for the Study of Civil Rights in Education opens in the former Moton High School on the Fiftieth Anniversary of the school strike for equal facilities for black students in Prince Edward County.

2003

Prince Edward County holds a symbolic (honorary) graduation ceremony for the "lost generation"—those denied education when schools were closed to resist integration between 1959 and 1964. (About 400 students attended). This was repeated the following year with the attendance of nearly 200 additional students.

2005

A commission was established by Governor Warner and the Virginia Assembly to supervise a Civil Rights Memorial monument.

The first Brown v. Board of Education Scholarships passed by the General Assembly and signed into law by Governor Warner were awarded. Anyone directed by the closing of Prince Edward County Public Schools for five years may continue their education free.

2007

Attorney Oliver Hill, one of the attorneys who fought for the integration of Prince Edward County Schools in the Brown v Griffin case, known as the Brown v Board of Education - Mr. Oliver W. Hill died at 100 years old. The Virginia flag is flown at half-mast.

2008

The Virginia Civil Rights Memorial was officially dedicated and unveiled on Capitol Square by Former Governor Tim Kaine. An estimated 4,000 people witnessed the historic event.

2013
Moton Museum completed a $5.5 million renovation and open its first permanent exhibition, The Moton School Story: Children of Courage.

2015
A replica of the Tar Papered Shack was placed alongside the Moton Museum to duplicate the Tar Papered Shacks alongside the Robert R. Moton High School to help with the over crowdedness in the early 1950's. A ribbon cutting was held.

Three Civil Rights and Educational leaders were honored with a proclamation. The School Board and members of the community presented a legacy program of naming Barbara Rose Johns Auditorium, of the high school, Reverend L. Francis Griffin, Sr. Gymnasium, of the Middle School and Dr. James M. Anderson, Jr. School Board Meeting Room, of the School Board Office. Each accepted a proclamation. Joan Johns Cobbs spoke on her sister Barbara's behalf, Naja Griffin- Johnson spoke on her father's Reverend Francis L Griffin's behalf and Dr. Anderson presented his speech.

2016
Former student of Prince Edward County Public School, Megan Lee Clark made history of becoming the first Black and first woman ever sworn in as Commonwealth Attorney in Prince Edward County.

Other Former students that still resides in Prince Edward County preceded her. James Ghee, First Black Attorney, Travis Harris, First Black Sheriff, Wesley Reed followed Harris and current sheriff, Armstead (Chuckie) Reid, Vice Mayor and many more.

2017
General State Building on Capitol Square in Richmond, Virginia was named after Barbara Rose Johns.

Barbara Rose Johns Day became an official holiday in Virginia.

2018
Robert R. Moton/Prince Edward County School Alumni Association partnered with the Moton Museum to begin plans for designing a "Digital Wall of Names" of ALL children whom were enrolled in school during the time Prince Edward County Public Schools were closed in 1959.

2019
March 30, 2019 Oliver Hill, Sr. Historical Marker was placed on the grounds of the Moton Museum in Farmville, Virginia.

May 23, 24, 25
NAACP and Moton Museum presented the 65th Anniversary of Brown v. Board of Education, 60th Anniversary of Closing of Prince Edward Public Schools and 55th Anniversary of Griffin vs. County School Board of Prince Edward County.

2020

*60th Anniversary of Ruby Bridges desegregation of schools in Louisiana

55th Anniversary of the voting Rights Act

65th Anniversary of Rosa Parks and the Montgomery Bus Boycott

*65th Anniversary of the Brown 2 Decision

65th Anniversary of Emmett Till

Index

Photos and Credits

Jackson, Thomas, 105

Jefferson, Carrie, 36

Jenkins, John Lacy, 103

Johns, Barbara Rose, 14

Johnson, Stanley, 150

Johnson, Lillian Jordan, 44

Johnson, Doris Day Miller, 123

Johnson, Dorothy Paige, 169

Johnson, Cynthia, 162

Johnson, Joseph, 238

Johnson, Naja Griffin, 187

Jones, Marjorie West, 235

Jones, Robert, 73

Jones, Sophia H., 163

Jordan, Darlene Jenkins, 76

Jordan, Eloise Lockett, 58

Jordan, Larry L., 214

Jordan, Libby 44

Justice, Hope Sutton Watkins, 57

Ward, Sally, 61

Watkins, Christine Irving, 93

Watkins, Ruth, 54

Ward, Sally, 61

Watson, Jimmy, 81

Williams, Cathy Allen, 51

Wiley, Mattie Paige, 241

Wise Jr., Lawrence (Lloyd), 182

Womack, Charlotte Herndon, 42

ABOUT THE AUTHOR

 Rita Odom Moseley, the older of two children, was raised in the town of Farmville, Virginia, Prince Edward County, where she still resides. She was directly affected as a little girl, with more than 2,300 African American schoolmates and at least 350 white students by the five-year closing of the public schools in her home town.

Her story, and the experience of her schoolmates, is the basis for the book *Silence Broken*. She was attending Prince Edward County public school system in 1959 when local leaders forced the closure of the schools for five years rather than desegregating. She was without an opportunity to go to school and get an education for two years. During the third year, she went to Blacksburg Virginia, to attend what would now be considered a middle school, graduating as salutatorian. The next year she attended school at Christiansburg Industrial Institute, CII.

She lived with two elderly ladies, a mother and daughter who Rita's family did not know but took her in. Rita stayed with the mother while the daughter worked in another town during the week. The mother was nearly 81 years old, and died at the age of 107. Rita returned home to Prince Edward in 1963 and attended the free school program until 1964, when the public schools reopened. She graduated from Robert R. Moton High School two years late. She took classes at Southside Community College and Longwood College (University).

Her story has been told on radio stations, including; WURD-AM in Philadelphia. She has been featured in many newspapers in various states, including the local paper The Farmville Herald. In addition to that, she has been featured in magazines such as Education Week, Time, Time Uptown, Crisis and Soul, Retirement Living, as well on the cover of the School Board News, Faith and Politics where she met and had a picture taken with Icon Congressman John Lewis, and placed on the 2020 cover of Southside Cooperative Living magazine. She has been featured on AP News, ABC World News, NBC, CBS, CNN, Current Events and in a special documentary by MSNBC, to name a few. Her words were reiterated in the play "Open the Door Virginia," a choreodrama production performed by Dianne McIntyre at the Center for the Arts – Theater of the First Amendment at George Mason University. Her voice is one of the first heard in the documentary, "Locked Out": The Fall of Massive Resistance, featuring her, school mates and other school districts." Excerpts of her story are told in the following authors' book: Vonita White-Foster and Gerald Foster, Terrance Hicks, Christopher Bonastio, and Jill Titus.

Rita has served on various committees in support of education, including one that contacted over 400 people to receive honorary diplomas during a graduation program at Prince Edward County High School in 2003. She spoke at the General Assembly before the Full House of Delegates Education Committee in support of passing the Brown v. Board of Education Scholarship Fund.

It was passed by the General Assembly in 2005 with Prince Edward residents who had traveled to Richmond for the vote looking on, sponsored by the "Get on the Bus Campaign" I and II, in which John Stokes played a major part in organizing. The bill was later signed by then-

Governor Mark Warner. The campaign concluded with a celebration held at Longwood University, during which Rita, who was also a member of the Light of Reconciliation committee, was one of the speakers.

Rita has been selected to participate in panelist discussions at the State Library of Virginia that kicked off the celebration of the unveiling of the Civil Rights Memorial Monument in Richmond. She was one of the panelists for a Civil Rights event at the University of Virginia Center for Politics, where she and others shared the stage with Sarah Collins Randolph, a survivor of the 10th Street bombing in Birmingham, a panelist for members of congress, who visited Farmville on a Three-Day Pilgrimage sponsored by the Faith & Politics Institute.

She was appointed by then-Governor Tim Kaine to serve on The Civil Rights Memorial Commission from 2006-2008 that selected a design by famous Paris sculptor Stanley Bleifeld. The four-sided memorial erected on the State Capitol Grounds honors the student protest at the Robert Russa Moton High School in Farmville, Virginia and she was a special guest to observe, her Majesty, "Queen Elizabeth's Walk Through" in Richmond, Virginia on May 3, 2003.

Rita is a member of the Saint Paul's College Alumni Association; the Moton and Prince Edward County Alumni Association; The National Association of Colored People, Moton Museum Volunteer, the Moton Museum Council and for years Committee Member of the Lest We Forget Scholarship Foundation, which gave scholarships to children of those directly affected by the closing of the schools in Prince Edward County.

You may also enjoy other books by
Rita Odom Moseley

No School

No School Second Edition

Lillie Mae Found Her School

Contact her at:

iamritaodommoseley@gmail.com

realistacs@yahoo.com

Made in the USA
Columbia, SC
02 December 2020